RACING

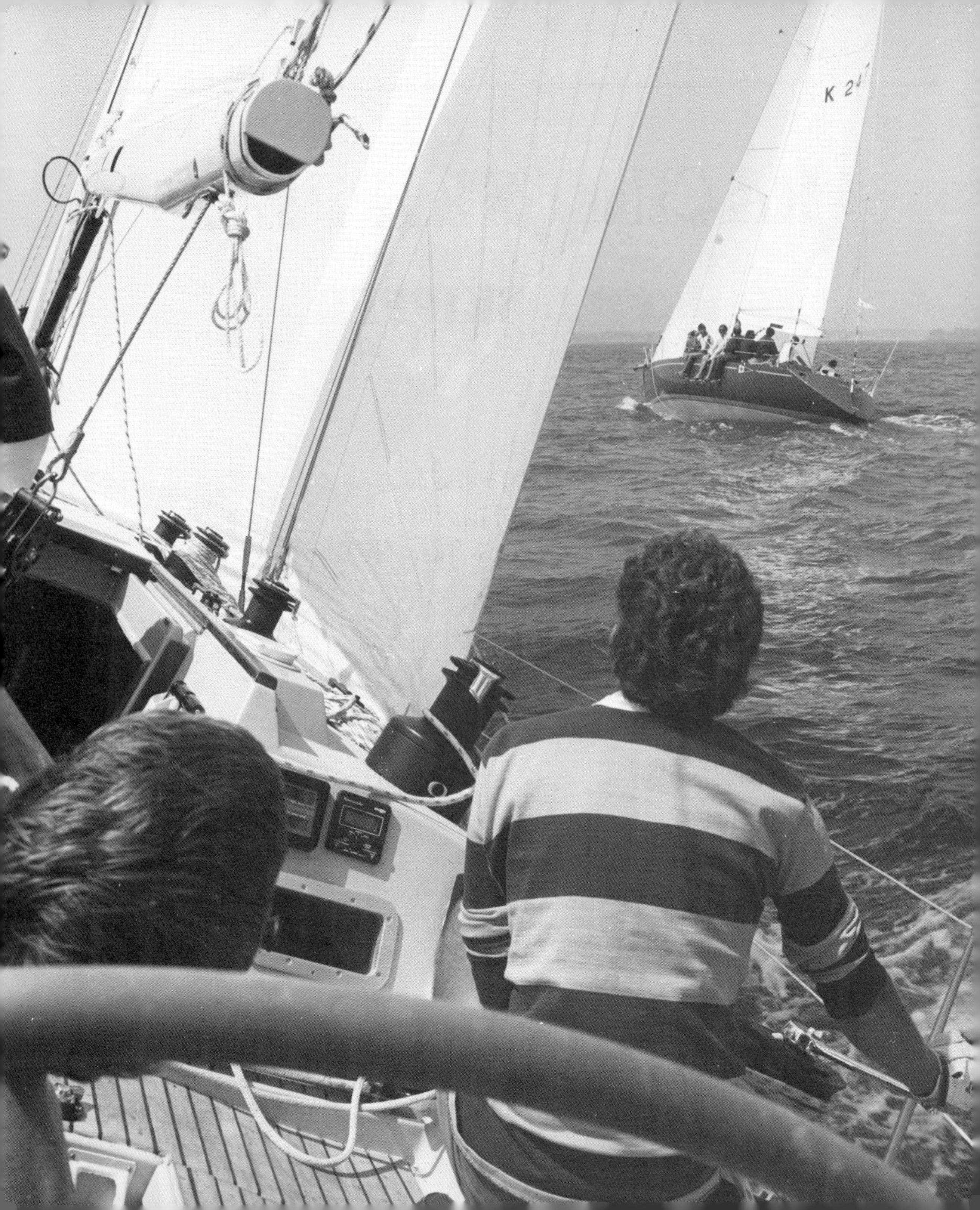

RACING SKIPPER

Robin Aisher
and Tim Davison
photographs by Tim Hore

Fernhurst Books

© Robin Aisher and Fernhurst Books 1985

First published 1985 by
Fernhurst Books, 33 Grand Parade
Brighton, East Sussex, BN2 2QA

All rights reserved. No part of this publication may be reproduced, stored in a retrieval system, or transmitted in any form or by any means, electronic, mechanical, photocopying, recording or otherwise, without the prior permission of Fernhurst Books.

ISBN 0 906754 69 0

Acknowledgements

The publishers wish to thank all those who offered advice on the contents list or on the manuscript: David Arnold, Julian Brooke-Houghton, Iain Macdonald-Smith, Andy Morley, Chris Preston, Crispin Reed-Wilson, and Nick Yoward.

Thanks are also due to all those who agreed to appear in the photographs: Caroline Aisher, Bill Edgerton, Derek Gill, Nick Haryett, Derek Ide, Mike Stansfeld, Bungy Taylor, Tony Vanderhasst and Bob Warren.

The polar table on pages 18-19 is reproduced by kind permission of Robert Humphreys Yacht Design, Lymington Marina, Bath Road, Lymington, Hampshire.

Permission is gratefully acknowledged to reproduce the following photographs: pages 9, 25, 31, 35, 53, 58-9, 69, 75, 79 — Roger Lean-Vercoe; pages 57, 61, 70, 72, 93 — William Payne. The cover photograph is by Eric North and the design is by Behram Kapadia.

Composition by A & G Phototypesetters, Knaphill
Printed by Ebenezer Baylis & Son Ltd, Worcester

Contents

Part 1 · Organising the boat
1 · Preparation *6*
2 · Before the race *21*
3 · During the race *24*
4 · Survival conditions *28*

Part 2 · Sailing the boat
5 · Starting to windward *30*
6 · Starting offwind *37*
7 · Beating in medium winds *41*
8 · Beating in light winds *51*
9 · Beating in strong winds *55*
10 · Tacking *60*
11 · The weather mark *64*
12 · Reaching *68*
13 · Gybing *74*
14 · The leeward mark *78*
15 · Running *80*
16 · Sailing at night *88*
17 · Offshore strategy *91*

1 · Preparation

Although this book is written with inshore and offshore racing in mind, it should also be useful to people who want to cruise smartly. Indeed, before buying a boat think first about what you are going to do with it. If your objective is mainly cruising with a few local races thrown in, you won't need a high-tech Admiral's Cupper. But if you are trying to win a national or world title your boat has to be the best available.

Let's suppose you are going for one major series and are determined to win. Ask yourself what sort of weather the regatta is likely to be sailed in. What size of boat is likely to do well? Should she have a fractional or masthead rig? Will a wheel or a tiller suit you best? Once you have answered these questions (which are discussed in more detail below) you can decide whether to build a new boat or modify an existing one.

Regatta venue? Look at the weather pattern over the race area; your local Met office should have the data you need going back several years. If it is likely to be a light-weather regatta you may need to lighten the boat and/or add more sail (note that a bigger mainsail is not too expensive in terms of rating). The existing sails may also need to be re-cut for the light conditions. But if it is likely to blow you should consider stiffening the boat (by adding ballast).

Size of boat? The selectors for a team don't usually choose boats all the same size. Find out what the other boats will be like, then choose yours carefully to fit into a gap.

Fractional vs masthead?
- A masthead rig is better for short tacking (because you regain power quicker).
- A masthead rig gives better pointing ability.
- A masthead rig is better downwind in light airs (because of its large spinnaker).
- A fractional rig is more adaptable upwind (it can be tuned like a dinghy).
- A fractional rig is faster on the reach (the rig delivers more power).
- A fractional rig is more stable downwind in a breeze.
- A fractional rig carries smaller headsails (less weight on board, and less expense).

So in crowded tidal areas where you have to beat up a narrow 'groove', the masthead rig scores because you can short-tack effectively and outpoint the boats around you. But in more open waters the fractional rig has a slight edge.

Wheel vs tiller? There is no doubt a tiller is best for 'feel' upwind, but downwind in a breeze it's murder (you may need three people on it to keep the boat straight). You pays your money and takes your choice — personally I prefer a wheel provided it is big enough (on 'Yeoman' it is 6 ft 3 in (1.9 m) in diameter) and properly geared (one turn of the wheel from lock to lock).

Building a new boat

If you can get away with modifying an existing boat — well and good. Often, though, there is nothing suitable and you are forced to build afresh.

Many owners are criticised for launching a new boat too late before a major event. In practice the best time to begin building is about 10 months before the

OPPOSITE *Masthead or fractional rig? See text for the advantages of each.*

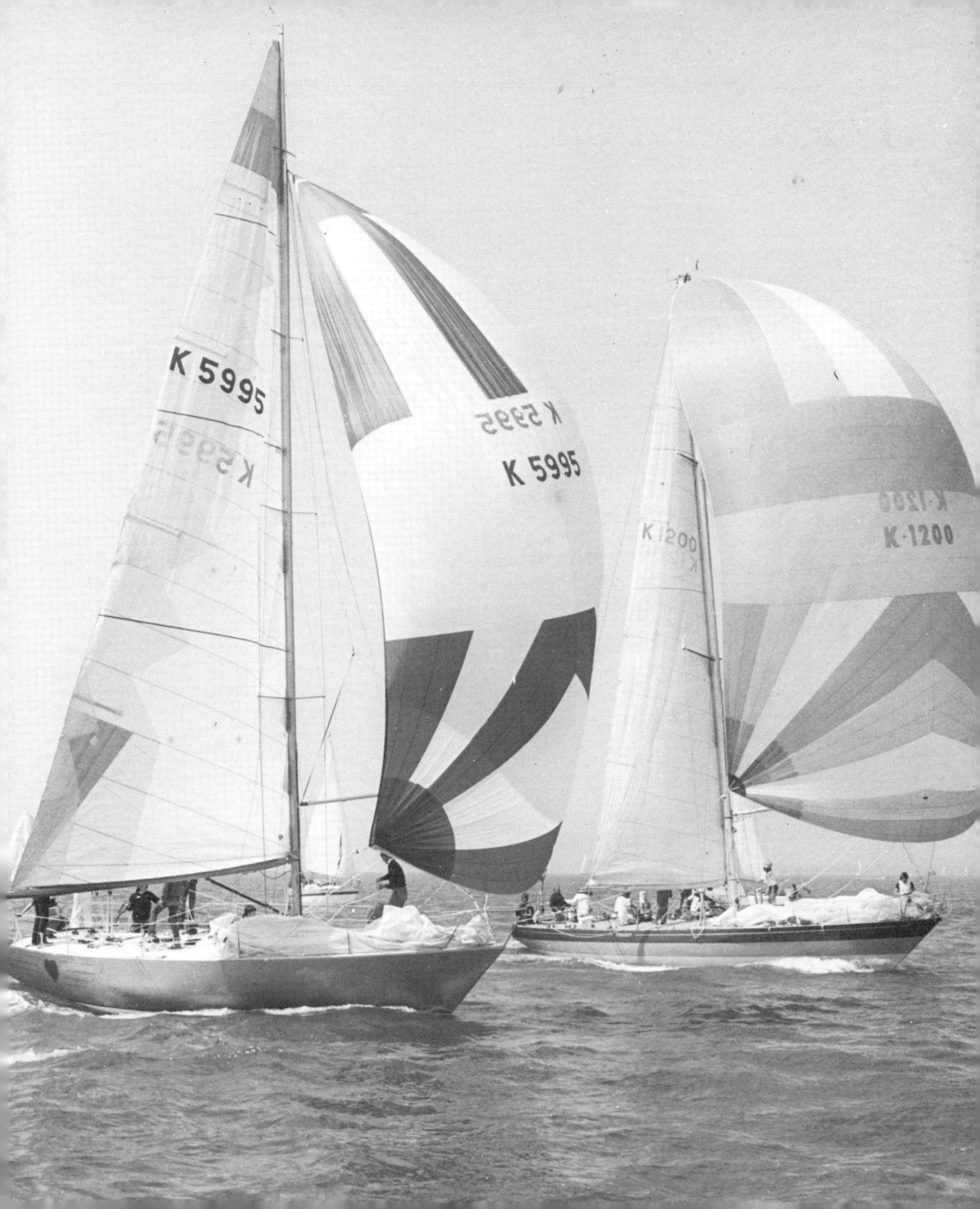
K 5995
K 5995
K 1200
K·1200

race — this makes sure your design incorporates the most recent changes in the IOR, minimises your chance of missing a design breakthrough but still gives enough time for the boat to be worked up.

Despite this, the campaign needs to start 18 months before the event (the table shows how this might work for the run-up to the Admiral's Cup). In the early stages you're just scuttlebutting, i.e. finding out as much as you can about everything that might affect the campaign, and in particular looking at various designers and checking how well their boats have done in recent races. We also try to see the direction the designer is going — maybe his latest designs are sacrificing downwind stability for upwind speed. This won't do if the series we're going for is expected to be windy — a boat that broaches all over the place would be lethal. In any case a boat that's relatively easy to sail is essential in this game because of the short time allocated to working her up.

Having settled on a designer and a method of construction, book your slot immediately at the builders — this will save many headaches later. Note from the table that the design is started in April but it is modified over the following few months in the light of racing results (such as the One Ton Cup). Building then begins in September or October for a February launch.

Timetable for an Admiral's Cup campaign

Jan	} Scuttlebutting	Jan	Building
Feb		Feb	Launching
Mar		Mar	Inshore testing
Apr	Begin design	Apr	Offshore testing
May	} Modify design	May	} Trial races
Jun		Jun	
July		July	} Admiral's Cup
Aug		Aug	
Sep	} Building		
Oct			
Nov			
Dec			

Building a crew

'Yeoman' needs a crew of 12 and there is usually a nucleus of 5 or 6 left from the previous campaign. We have our first crew meeting as soon as the design for the new boat has been drawn, so that each person can check his area and redesign if necessary. Having items such as the deck layout agreed at this stage saves innumerable gripes later.

If there is a local winter series we usually borrow a boat and try out potential crew members. For the latest campaign we tried 32 people before selecting the final 15 (15 rather than 12 to give some reserves, not everyone being able to come each weekend). Essentially we are looking for people who:

- Can sail.
- Can get on socially.
- Are experts in their area (we chose a world-class Contender sailor to trim our mainsail — a Contender only *has* a main so it was obvious he could do the job!)
- Are (or can be) convinced that the job they are doing on board is the job they want to do (it's no good choosing a navigator who'd rather be helming).
- Are 'adrenalin runners' — i.e. thrive under pressure and won't collapse on the big day.

We reckon that each crewman has five jobs:
1. Modifying the design so he is sure his part of the boat will work.
2. Visiting the boat during construction to check the design is being interpreted properly (this also enthuses the builder, who likes to feel part of the team).
3. Making changes as the boat is worked up.
4. Crewing during the race.
5. Doing an alternative job, e.g. electrician, social organiser.

Having assembled a good crew, the next problem is keeping them together. The best solution is . . . to keep winning! But if the early season's results are poor your job is to convince the team that the boat *will* win, and that you are working at it.

Two people are vital to the organisation of the boat and crew. The first is the boat's *coordinator*; on our boat he is the deputy helmsman too: There is such a

ABOVE: I prefer a wheel to a tiller provided it is large enough — on 'Yeoman' the wheel is 1.9 m in diameter.

lot of legwork involved in running a large boat that it is virtually impossible for the skipper to do it all — he may be the chairman but he needs a managing director to take some of the load. The coordinator should be an in-depth sailor, interested in new designs and gear for the boat, capable of choosing the best sailmaker and working with him, keeping a list of potential crewmen, and so on. He should be someone the skipper can talk to, and also someone for the crew to sound out before they approach the skipper.

The second key person is the *crew boss*. He is the Chief Petty Officer, and his job is to unify the work of everyone on deck (including the helmsman). Whilst the skipper has the ultimate responsibility for everything — liaising with the navigator, checking the lights are working, deciding on race strategy — the crew boss makes sure the right sails are on deck, that everyone knows how they should be hoisted and what each person should do. He needs to be forceful, knowledgeable and understanding (there is no point in shouting at someone who is doing his best). With the crew under his wing, everyone else can get on with sailing the boat, freed from worrying about the antics on the foredeck.

It is very helpful if one of the crew is a sailmaker because they are really the best people to train the trimmers. It also guarantees first call on repair facilities — very handy when you need a damaged sail back for next weekend's race.

The campaign

Once the boat is launched she is sailed every weekend. With an amateur crew it is not feasible to

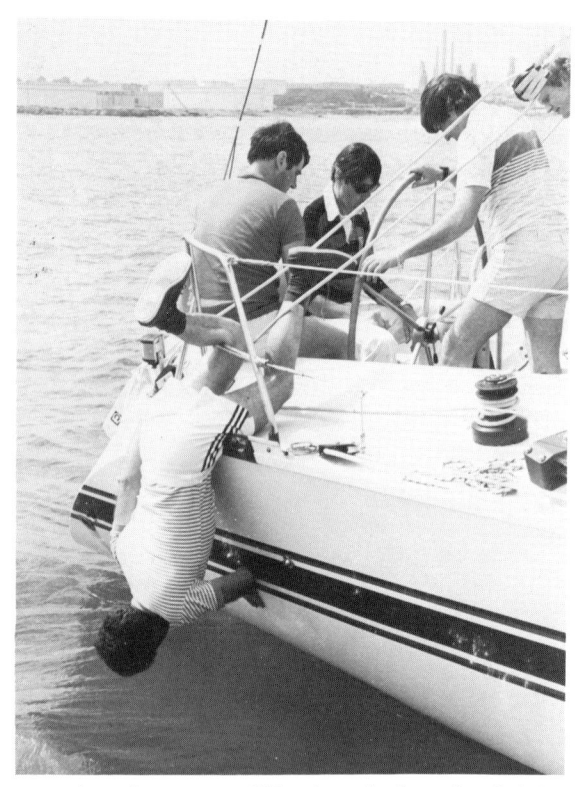

ABOVE A good crewman will bend over backwards to help!

sail midweek, though the boat might well go out with a scratch crew to check sail alterations or to make sure a new system works.

Inshore races are used to try out new things because it is easier to see what is going on when other boats are close.

We also meet once or twice a week to chew the fat: any crewman is welcome to come and talk or listen but the helmsman, tactician, boat coordinator, sailmaker and designer are needed every time.

It's also very useful to team up with another boat your size and sail together before and after races to experiment.

Do encourage the crew to comment after each race — both while sailing home (if a manoeuvre went wrong you can practise it right away) and ashore. The guys on the weather rail often spot things, particularly on the opposition's boats, that the afterguard miss completely.

Finally, make sure you have a friendly yard. If you order an alteration on a Monday you must know that it will be done by Friday, and to a high standard. A good yard lives by your boat — in return, any success you have will rub off on them.

The necessities of life

If the food, drink or fuel run out offshore your name will be mud. Here are a few rules of thumb to help avoid embarrassment.

Water. Since water is heavy the tank is placed to give the best rating. You can never have too much water and dehydration slows the crew down dramatically. As a minimum take 2 pints (1 litre) per person per day, plus a further 5 gallons (23 litres).

Drinks. We have no alcohol on 'Yeoman' (save for one 'medicinal' bottle, which is somehow always emptied between the finish line and shore). Alcohol doesn't stimulate — it is a depressant and blurs the judgement, particularly in the small hours. The crew do *not* need a drink to keep going.

By way of atonement there should be a constant supply of Coca Cola, shandy and lime juice to hand, plus hot drinks. On 'Yeoman' these are organised on the 'travel pack' principle: cardboard cups containing powder are filled from Thermos flasks of hot water, so anyone can have a hot drink of his choice at any time. For those occasions when everyone is thirsty there is a tray with 12 holes cut in it so 12 cups can be passed up at once. The tray fits on the gimbals down below.

Food. Food is important for both performance and morale. To ensure a balanced diet someone has to be in charge of planning the meals for the trip. In our case it is an outside caterer who packages meals so they simply have to be heated up; stews (in pots) and variety of dishes in aluminium trays (take-away style) work well. If you have a freezer on board the pots and trays are easy to store; if not, take them straight from the deep-freeze ashore into an insulated box, which is then carried on the boat. Note that the box is loaded in reverse order, i.e. Monday's meals on top of Tuesday's.

We keep our mealtimes absolutely regular, because this helps everyone pace themselves. But snacks are available anytime; we favour nuts, raisins, figs and chocolate bars because they are 'go fast' foods, packed with carbohydrate.

Fuel

We normally run the engine for four hours each day to generate power. The main criterion is sufficient fuel for this rather than enough to get home from the furthest point of the trip. In practice we normally sail with about 5 gallons (23 litres) of diesel.

ABOVE Food is important for performance . . . and morale.

Instruments

I firmly believe yachts should make good use of the new technology. Not only do instruments make sailing safer, they add a new challenge and make offshore sailing far more fun: when there are no other boats in sight you still have the instruments to race against.

There is a bewildering range of instruments available. The sections below list the types of instruments and what each does. In case you don't want your bulkhead to look like an aircraft console I've asterisked the ones I feel are essential for racing.

Before launching into the list, here are a few general points to bear in mind.

- You should never rely entirely on instruments. On one Sydney – Hobart race our impeller became clogged but Ambrose Greenway was able to navigate the whole race using a sextant. We always carry one now — even when Ambrose is not on board!
- If your instruments have a damping facility you will need to adjust this according to the conditions. Although the readings are more accurate with a lot of damping, you can't always afford the associated time lag. So:

  Inshore, turn the damping down. You will be steering the boat a lot (short-tacking is the extreme example) and can't afford to wait for the instruments to catch up. It is a nasty feeling to see the speed apparently dropping as you accelerate out of a tack. Turn the damping down.

  Offshore, accuracy is the chief aim to help the crew hit maximum boatspeed. So increase the damping facility to stop the values oscillating as you bounce over waves.

- Some instruments are sensitive to voltage fluctuations, so it is as well to carry a voltmeter on board.

Compass. Make sure your compass
- Is steady
- Is big enough to steer by.
- Will work at any angle of heel.
- Is gorilla proof (a careless crewman with a winch handle will soon dispose of a weak compass).
- Has three lubber lines (for steering from either deck and from amidships).
- Is borne in mind when stowage of metal objects is being arranged (a rack for winch handles beneath the compass is not helpful).
- Is swung (if you suspect the instrument, sail along a charted transit and compare the compass bearing with the charted bearing).

On 'Yeoman' we have a traditional and a digital

compass. As helmsman I use the traditional one downwind and the digital read-outs upwind. (Do remember, however, that you should rarely steer a compass course when racing — following the wind and waves is far more important.) The navigator uses the digital display all the time. Note that the rules state you must carry more than one compass when racing offshore.

Boatspeed read-out (and log coupling). An accurate speed read-out is essential for racing. It is impossible to tune the boat without it because you're dealing with such small speed differences. One-tenth of a knot, for example, will put you 1.5 *miles* ahead at the end of a 100-mile race! Make sure your boatspeed read-out
- Is digital (analogue dials are hopeless).
- Reads to one (or preferably two) decimal places.
- Has the correct amount of damping (see above).

Boatspeed is your entry to the wonderful world of the *polar table*, which can revolutionise your sailing. More of this later in the chapter.

The log is built into the speedo.
- The log should be digital.
- The spinner should be easy to get at (it is bound to become clogged with seaweed).
- Do carry a spare spinner in case of damage. (Try at all costs to avoid streaming a 'conventional' log — the drag is phenomenal.) If your log is suspect, check it by sailing over a measured course.

Wind direction read-out. It is vital to know the wind direction accurately when sailing off the wind. The wind indicator is useful, of course, but in a sea-

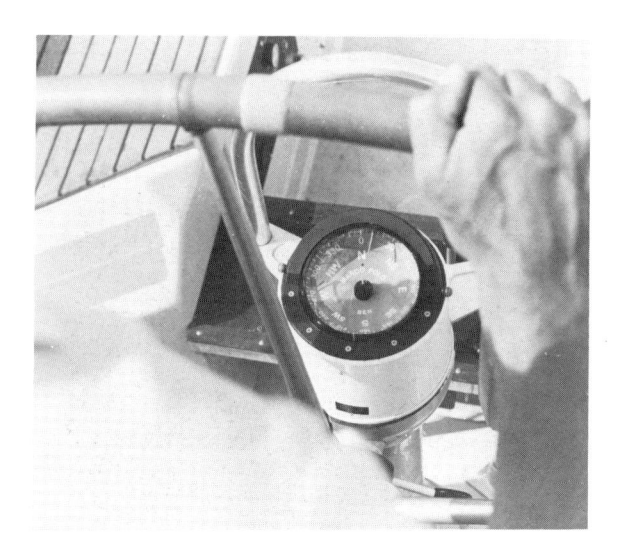

way it bounces around too much for precision. Wind direction is needed so you can:
- Decide which sails to set.
- Find the best wind angle for downwind sailing.
- Know what angle to gybe through.
- Calculate the true wind direction (and then work out the wind on the next leg).
- Use your polar table.

But when beating, ignore the read-out and use the telltales on the genoa — they are a far more accurate gauge of wind direction, even at night.

***Windspeed read-out (apparent).** At the very least the windspeed tells you when it is blowing too hard to leave the marina! It also helps you:
- Calculate the true wind speed. This is very useful for navigational purposes (it confirms that a front is coming through, a sea breeze is building, etc.).
- Decide when to change sails.
- Use your polar table.

***Depth meter.** Make sure your depth meter
- Has a read-out on deck.
- Is accurate to one decimal place.
- Works when the boat is heeling (as it will be most of the time). Some types indicate you have plenty of water when the boat is lying over but she hits the bottom when you tack and the keel comes upright.

In most waters a deep-reading gauge is not needed. But in certain parts of the world they are essential — off Tasmania, for instance the key tactic is to run down the edge of the ocean shelf for maximum stream, and the depth gauge needs to go to 200 fathoms (365 metres).

Before sophisticated navigation systems like Decca appeared on the scene we used to navigate

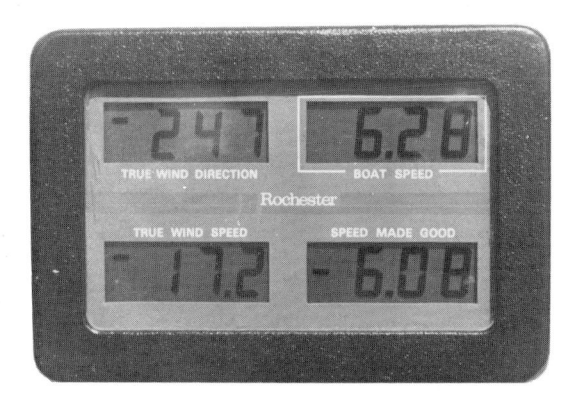

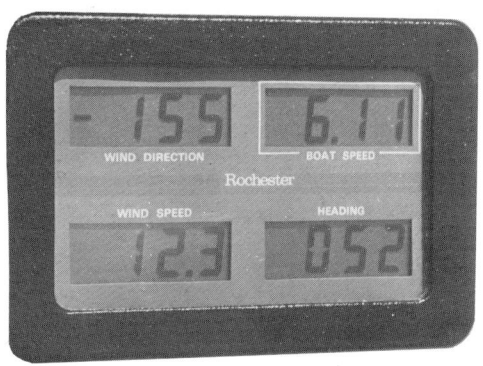

Instruments. Our instruments are mounted in the helmsman's line of sight (LEFT). FAR LEFT A traditional compass is most useful downwind. ABOVE This panel shows true windspeed and direction, boatspeed and VMG. ABOVE, RIGHT Depth meter. RIGHT This panel displays compass bearing (heading), apparent windspeed and direction, and boatspeed once again.

using depth of water, and it is still a very good way to find your way around. Though I must admit that the navigator on 'Yeoman' used to be a submariner, so I may be a bit biased.

There's only one way to calibrate the depth meter accurately — sail up to some soft sand, run the boat aground and take a reading as she touches.

***Radio** It is essential to have a really good radio with long, short, medium and FM bands. Apart from keeping the crew entertained, the main use is catching weather forecasts — and not just the main national forecasts but also the local ones. "It will be a hot sunny day on the beaches of Cornwall" is vital sea-breeze information on the Fastnet.

Inclinometer. We use two inclinometers: one mounted across the boat and one aligned fore-and-aft. The athwartships one is a useful aid:
- To help decide when to change sails. Windspeed is not the only factor: if you are heeling excessively, you will go faster with less sail up.
- To help the navigator predict leeway. The fore-and-aft inclinometer is set up on the dock in sailing trim. It is used as a reference point when sailing (see chapters 7, 8, 9 and 15).

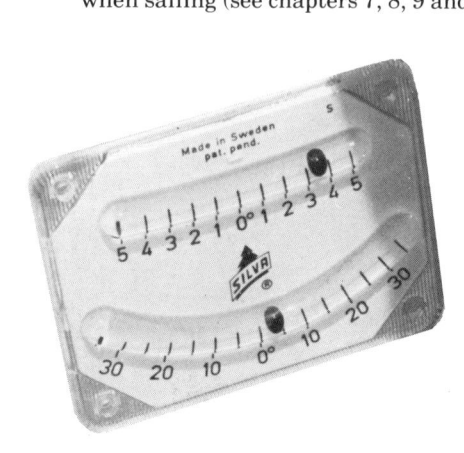

This inclinometer has two scales. The fine scale is used if the instrument is mounted fore-and-aft; the coarse scale is used if it is set athwartships.

Sextant. In case all else fails.

Barograph. Shows trends in air pressure. Although pressure changes are given on the radio, a visual read-out is more helpful.

Thermometer. Very useful for detecting changes in the Gulf Stream. Simply flush the heads a few times, and insert the thermometer.

Electronics

The instruments I've looked at so far are all a competent navigator needs. He can use them to work out true windspeed and direction, VMG, and a host of other data.

The advent of electronics has simply freed him from having to do these calculations — the instruments give the results instantly and effortlessly.

On 'Yeoman' the read-outs can be changed from apparent to true at the touch of a switch.

True wind direction read-out. We use the true wind direction read-out a great deal. It is particularly useful at night, when it is easy to get disorientated.

Before the start the wind direction and the line bearing are compared every few minutes to find the favoured end of the startline.

Before (and during) the race a plot of true wind direction against time shows the pattern of the windshifts. This can either be plotted manually, or by the computer on a VDU.

Wind direction is a useful meteorological tool. It shows when the boat has reached a wind bend (caused by the land, perhaps), when the sea breeze is making itself felt, and when fronts are having an effect.

True wind speed read-out. In light airs it is comforting to know whether the wind across the deck is caused by the boat's motion or if it is a real breeze.

Knowing the true windspeed helps you choose the right sails, particularly before the start (when you may not have time to sail up the first leg) and when deciding on sails for the next leg.

ABOVE *The navigatorium on 'Yeoman XXIV' contains, among other electronic aids, the Decca system, the Weatherfax machine, and an Apple computer (*BELOW*) which is being used here to compare the required course and the actual course made good.*

PREPARATION

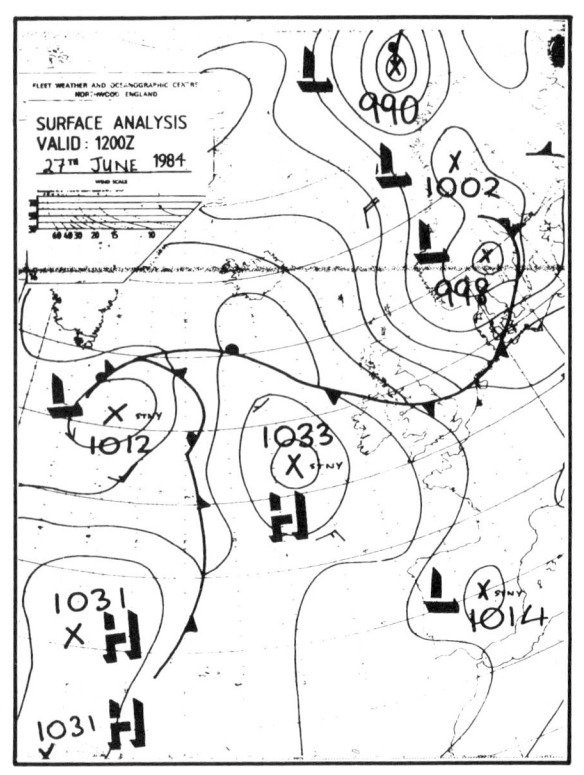

Figure 1.1

VMG read-out. VMG (velocity made good) gives a direct measure of your performance when beating and running. Use of this read-out is covered in chapters 7 and 15.

Automatically coupled direction finders (e.g. Decca, Satnav). These are very useful because they are so accurate. You can constantly update:
- Your position.
- Your course to the next mark.
- The distance to the next mark.
- How far off the rhumb line you are.
- What leeway you're making (or how far the tide has swept you).

You can also use the instrument to work out:
- If you are making progress against the tide (or should kedge).
- If you are dragging the anchor.
- If the tide has turned (sailing cross-tide, for example, your course will curve one way, then the other).
- How far you are from the startline (though this will never be as accurate as a transit).

Weatherfax. This machine prints a weather map (similar to the one given in the daily newspaper), with the advantage that you can choose the height

LEFT *The Weatherfax machine produces meterological printouts like that shown (reduced) in figure 1.1.* BELOW *The Decca system.*

16

above sea level you are interested in. This is a great help since what is happening at 10,000 feet (3000 metres) may soon be what we get at sea level. (Figure 1.1)

You may also be able to tune in to weather transmissions from other countries — very useful if you are racing towards a foreign shore.

Polar tables

Instruments are dynamite when used in conjunction with a polar table. This is a chart which gives the best possible boatspeed for a variety of wind strengths and angles, and can vary from a simple home-made affair to a complex computer-generated job.

Making a polar table. Provided you have some instruments (boatspeed, apparent windspeed and apparent wind angle) you can make your own polar table. Draw up a blank chart (figure 1.2) and then simply fill in the best speeds recorded as you sail. You can do this both in practice (sail at a variety of angles to the wind, recording speeds as you go) and during the race, but do make sure that the speed you record is the optimum; everyone should have their boots over the side, the sails must be trimmed properly and the helmsman fully 'in the groove'.

Using the table. Offshore, and particularly at night, there is usually nothing to race against except the figures on the table. We keep several plastic-covered copies of the table on board, and use them as our bible.

1 Get on course and work the boat up to maximum speed.
2 Record this boatspeed.
3 Look up the optimum speed on the table. If you are slow, make an adjustment to the trim or the rig.
4 Wait at least 30 seconds before checking the

Figure 1.2

APPARENT WINDSPEED (KNOTS)

APPARENT WIND ANGLE (OFF BOW)

	0	1	2	3	4	5	6	7	8	9	10	11	12	13	----	30
20°																
25°																
30°																
35°																
40°																
45°																
50°																
55°																
60°																
65°																
⋮																
180°																

YEOMAN XXIII - POLAR

TRUE WIND SPEED

		3	4	5	6	7	8	9	10	11	12	13
40°	BOATSPEED	2.40	3.14	3.83	4.45	4.95	5.37	5.73	6.03	6.28	6.46	6.6
	APP. W. ANGLE	22.1	22.3	22.5	22.7	22.9	23.2	23.4	23.7	23.9	24.2	24.5
	APP. W. SPEED	5.03	6.65	8.22	9.71	11.08	12.36	13.58	14.73	15.83	16.87	17.8
45°	BOATSPEED	2.72	3.54	4.30	4.94	5.48	5.94	6.31	6.58	6.77	6.92	7.0
	APP. W. ANGLE	23.4	23.6	24.0	24.2	24.5	25.1	25.5	26.0	26.4	26.8	
	APP. W. SPEED	5.24	6.93	8.50	10.01	11.37	12.63	13.82	14.92	15.94	16.91	17.8
50°	BOATSPEED	2.99	3.88	4.68	5.35	5.94	6.42	6.73	6.94	7.10	7.21	7.3
	APP. W. ANGLE	24.8	25.1	25.5	25.9	26.3	26.5	27.0	27.6	28.1	28.6	29.1
	APP. W. SPEED	5.38	7.09	8.70	10.17	11.54	12.77	13.87	14.88	15.82	16.75	17.5
55°	BOATSPEED	3.21	4.16	4.98	5.70	6.33	6.75	7.00	7.17	7.30	7.40	7.4
	APP. W. ANGLE	26.2	26.6	27.1	27.6	28.0	28.4	29.0	29.7	30.3	30.9	31.4
	APP. W. SPEED	5.47	7.18	8.77	10.25	11.62	12.78	13.76	14.68	15.54	16.37	17.16
60°	BOATSPEED	3.40	4.38	5.22	5.97	6.58	6.94	7.17	7.32	7.43	7.52	7.5
	APP. W. ANGLE	27.6	28.1	28.8	29.4	29.9	30.7	31.4	32.0	32.7	33.3	34.0
	APP. W. SPEED	5.50	7.21	8.77	10.24	11.56	12.62	13.53	14.35	15.15	15.90	16.6
65°	BOATSPEED	3.55	4.55	5.40	6.18	6.74	7.07	7.28	7.43	7.52	7.60	7.6
	APP. W. ANGLE	29.1	29.8	30.6	31.2	32.0	33.0	33.9	34.5	35.1	35.9	36.9
	APP. W. SPEED	5.48	7.16	8.69	10.15	11.37	12.37	13.22	13.97	14.68	15.4	16.13
70°	BOATSPEED	3.65	4.67	5.53	6.33	6.85	7.16	7.36	7.50	7.59	7.65	7.7
	APP. W. ANGLE	30.7	31.5	32.5	33.10	34.2	35.4	36.4	37.1	37.7	38.7	40.0
	APP. W. SPEED	5.42	7.05	8.55	9.97	11.12	12.06	12.85	13.54	14.17	14.87	15.5
75°	BOATSPEED	3.72	4.75	5.63	6.43	6.92	7.22	7.41	7.55	7.64	7.69	7.7
	APP. W. ANGLE	32.4	33.3	34.4	35.2	36.5	37.8	38.9	39.8	40.5	41.8	43
	APP. W. SPEED	5.31	6.90	8.36	9.73	10.81	11.69	12.44	13.08	13.63	14.32	15.0
80°	BOATSPEED	3.77	4.80	5.69	6.49	6.97	7.26	7.45	7.59	7.68	7.74	7.8
	APP. W. ANGLE	34.2	35.1	36.3	37.30	38.8	40.3	41.6	42.6	43.4	45.0	46.5
	APP. W. SPEED	5.17	6.72	8.12	9.44	10.46	11.30	12.00	12.59	13.09	13.77	14.4
85°	BOATSPEED	3.78	4.82	5.72	6.52	7.00	7.29	7.49	7.63	7.72	7.80	7.8
	APP. W. ANGLE	36.0	37.2	38.4	39.4	41.1	42.9	44.4	45.6	46.5	48.3	49
	APP. W. SPEED	4.99	6.47	7.85	9.12	10.08	10.87	11.54	12.10	12.57	13.22	13.8
170°	BOATSPEED	1.65	2.19	2.72	3.24	3.76	4.26	4.74	5.21	5.67	6.13	6.5
	APP. W. ANGLE	157.9	157.9	158.1	158.2	158.4	158.6	158.9	159.1	159.4	159.5	159
	APP. W. SPEED	1.36	1.81	2.28	2.76	3.23	3.74	4.26	4.79	5.32	5.85	6.4
175°	BOATSPEED	1.57	2.09	2.60	3.10	3.59	4.07	4.54	4.99	5.43	5.87	6.3
	APP. W. ANGLE	169.4	169.4	169.4	169.5	169.6	169.7	169.8	169.9	170.0	170.1	170
	APP. W. SPEED	1.39	1.86	2.34	2.82	3.32	3.82	4.34	4.88	5.42	5.97	6.51
180°	BOATSPEED	1.50	2.00	2.49	2.97	3.44	3.91	4.36	4.80	5.23	5.65	6.0
	APP. W. ANGLE	180.0	180.0	180.0	180.0	180.0	180.0	180.0	180.0	180.0	180.0	180
	APP. W. SPEED	1.45	1.93	2.42	2.92	3.44	3.95	4.48	5.03	5.58	6.14	6
OPTIMUM VMG UP-WIND	BOATSPEED	2.85	3.68	4.39	4.97	5.51	5.99	6.24	6.40	6.51	6.59	6.6
	APP. W. ANGLE	24.1	24.3	24.3	24.4	24.7	25.0	24.9	24.8	24.7	24.7	24.8
	APP. W. SPEED	5.31	6.98	8.56	10.01	11.37	12.65	13.81	14.89	15.90	16.90	17.8
DOWN-WIND	BOATSPEED	2.02	2.65	3.26	3.86	4.41	4.93	5.46	6.02	6.43	6.73	6.9
	APP. W. ANGLE	110.5	112.3	114.4	115.9	118.0	121.1	122.7	122.4	127.0	134.4	140
	APP. W. SPEED	1.55	2.06	2.56	3.07	3.58	4.07	4.60	5.18	5.62	6.05	6.5
		3	4	5	6	7	8	9	10	11	12	13

IOR DATA FROM CERTIFICATE DATED 24/6/82, R=34.1

ROB

Figure 1.3

BLE

15	16	17	18	19	20	21	22	23	24	25		
6.80	6.84	6.89	6.93	6.97	7.00	7.02	7.04	7.06	7.07	7.07	BOATSPEED	
25.0	25.4	25.8	26.1	26.4	26.7	26.9	27.2	27.3	27.5	27.6	APP.W.ANGLE	40°
19.75	20.63	21.49	22.35	23.21	24.05	24.9	25.73	26.53	27.34	28.15	APP.W.SPEED	
6.17	7.23	7.27	7.31	7.34	7.36	7.38	7.40	7.41	7.42	7.42	BOATSPEED	
27.5	27.9	28.2	28.6	28.9	29.1	29.5	29.7	30.0	30.3	30.5	APP.W.ANGLE	45°
19.63	20.46	21.28	22.09	22.9	23.7	24.5	25.3	26.09	26.87	27.65	APP.W.SPEED	
6.42	7.46	7.49	7.52	7.55	7.56	7.58	7.59	7.60	7.61	7.61	BOATSPEED	
29.8	30.3	30.8	31.3	31.7	32.1	32.5	32.9	33.2	33.5	33.8	APP.W.ANGLE	50°
19.21	20.03	20.82	21.6	22.39	23.17	23.94	24.71	25.47	26.24	26.99	APP.W.SPEED	
7.56	7.60	7.62	7.65	7.67	7.69	7.70	7.71	7.72	7.72	7.73	BOATSPEED	
32.6	33.2	33.8	34.4	34.9	35.4	35.8	36.2	36.6	37.0	37.4	APP.W.ANGLE	55°
18.73	19.5	20.27	21.03	21.78	22.54	23.29	24.04	24.79	25.53	26.27	APP.W.SPEED	
7.65	7.68	7.71	7.73	7.75	7.77	7.79	7.80	7.81	7.82	7.82	BOATSPEED	
35.6	36.3	37.0	37.7	38.2	38.8	39.3	39.8	40.3	40.7	41.1	APP.W.ANGLE	60°
18.17	18.92	19.66	20.40	21.14	21.88	22.62	23.35	24.08	24.83	25.54	APP.W.SPEED	
7.72	7.75	7.78	7.80	7.83	7.84	7.86	7.88	7.89	7.91	7.92	BOATSPEED	
38.8	39.6	40.4	41.1	41.8	42.4	43.0	43.6	44.1	44.6	45.1	APP.W.ANGLE	65°
17.59	18.32	19.04	19.77	20.50	21.22	21.94	22.67	23.39	24.11	24.83	APP.W.SPEED	
7.78	7.81	7.84	7.87	7.90	7.93	7.95	7.97	7.99	8.01	8.03	BOATSPEED	
42.1	43.0	43.9	44.70	45.5	46.2	46.9	47.5	48.1	48.6	49.1	APP.W.ANGLE	70°
17.0	17.71	18.42	19.15	19.86	20.58	21.29	22.01	22.73	23.44	24.16	APP.W.SPEED	
7.84	7.88	7.92	7.96	7.99	8.03	8.06	8.09	8.12	8.14	8.17	BOATSPEED	
45.6	46.6	47.6	48.5	49.3	50.1	50.8	51.5	52.1	52.7	53.3	APP.W.ANGLE	75°
16.41	17.11	17.82	18.53	19.24	19.96	20.67	21.38	22.09	22.8	23.51	APP.W.SPEED	
7.91	7.96	8.01	8.06	8.10	8.14	8.18	8.22	8.25	8.28	8.31	BOATSPEED	
49.1	50.3	51.3	52.3	53.2	54.1	54.8	55.6	56.2	56.9	57.5	APP.W.ANGLE	80°
15.83	16.53	17.24	17.94	18.64	19.35	20.04	20.75	21.44	22.14	22.83	APP.W.SPEED	
8.00	8.06	8.12	8.17	8.22	8.27	8.31	8.35	8.38	8.42	8.45	BOATSPEED	
52.8	54.0	55.2	56.2	57.2	58.1	59.0	59.8	60.5	61.2	61.8	APP.W.ANGLE	85°
15.27	15.95	16.64	17.33	18.02	18.70	19.4	20.09	20.76	21.45	22.14	APP.W.SPEED	

15	16	17	18	19	20	21	22	23	24	25		
7.22	7.48	7.72	7.94	8.15	8.35	8.55	8.74	8.93	9.11	9.30	BOATSPEED	
160.7	161.2	161.6	162.0	162.4	162.8	163.1	163.4	163.6	163.8	164.0	APP.W.ANGLE	170°
7.73	8.45	9.20	9.96	10.73	11.52	12.30	13.10	13.89	14.69	15.48	APP.W.SPEED	
7.03	7.30	7.54	7.77	8.00	8.18	8.37	8.55	8.74	8.92	9.10	BOATSPEED	
170.5	170.7	170.9	171.1	171.3	171.5	171.6	171.7	171.9	172.0	172.1	APP.W.ANGLE	175°
7.77	8.47	9.21	9.97	10.75	11.53	12.32	13.11	13.91	14.71	15.52	APP.W.SPEED	
6.83	7.12	7.37	7.60	7.81	8.01	8.20	8.39	8.57	8.74	8.92	BOATSPEED	
180.0	180.0	180.0	180.0	180.0	180.0	180.0	180.0	180.0	180.0	180.0	APP.W.ANGLE	180°
7.91	8.60	9.33	10.09	10.86	11.64	12.43	13.23	14.03	14.84	15.65	APP.W.SPEED	

15	16	17	18	19	20	21	22	23	24	25			
6.77	6.81	6.86	6.90	6.93	6.97	7.00	7.02	7.03	7.04	7.05	BOATSPEED	UP-WIND	OPTIMUM VMG
25.0	25.3	25.6	25.9	26.2	26.5	26.7	27.0	27.2	27.4	27.5	APP.W.ANGLE		
19.74	20.62	21.49	22.36	23.21	24.06	24.91	25.74	26.55	27.36	28.16	APP.W.SPEED		
7.45	7.67	7.88	8.08	8.28	8.47	8.67	8.87	9.07	9.28	9.48	BOATSPEED	DOWN-WIND	
149.0	151.5	153.3	154.7	155.8	156.5	156.9	157.2	157.2	157.1	157.0	APP.W.ANGLE		
7.84	8.55	9.28	10.03	10.80	11.58	12.37	13.16	13.95	14.75	15.54	APP.W.SPEED		

15	16	17	18	19	20	21	22	23	24	25

HUMPHREYS YACHT DESIGN

boatspeed again — it will take at least this long for the alteration to have any effect.
5 If you are still slower than the table, make another adjustment (only make *one* adjustment at a time or you will become completely confused).
- If your speed is *better* than the table predicted, change the table to keep it showing the optimum. You are allowed to refine the table upwards, but never down!
- You can use the table to spot a good helmsman or trimmer.
- The table is essential for tuning a new mast or a new suit of sails (ideally you will be able to revise all the numbers upwards).
- You can also check sail deterioration during the season (it gradually becomes impossible to hit any of the numbers).

Computer-generated tables. It is now possible to send the lines of your boat to an agency that uses a computer to generate a theoretical polar table. I am sure this will become more common, and one day every owner will be given a polar table with his new boat. Figure 1.3 on pages 18-19 shows the table for 'Yeoman XXIII' produced by Robert Humphries. It is similar to figure 1.2 but note:
- It is laid out for true wind-speed and angle, since the boat has these read-outs. For example, if the wind is 6 knots (true) at 40 degrees (true) off the bow, we should be doing 4.45 knots (the apparent wind angle is 22.7 degrees and the apparent windspeed 9.71 knots in this case).
- There is a very useful section at the bottom showing optimum running angles and speeds. For example, at 10 knots true (5.18 knots apparent) we would sail at 122 degrees apparent and then try to build the speed up to 6.02 knots.
- The figures are theoretical. If the actual boatspeed is better than predicted of course we enter the higher figure. But if we fail to attain the theoretical value three times in a row and there are no obvious reasons why (dirty bottom, old sails, some of the crew below) then we might adjust the figure downwards.

Organisation ashore

One person should be detailed to look after the wellbeing of the crew ashore. Hotels need to be arranged, restaurants booked and supporters transported to the quay so they arrive just before the boat docks.

This is not an easy job, but if it's carried out well it plays an important part in building the crew's morale. If you leave things to chance you may have a thirsty, hungry and aggressive crew on your hands (and you may not be entirely satisfied yourself).

2 · Before the race

With a fast boat and an expert crew depending on them, the skipper and navigator need to plan each race carefully. In this chapter I want to look at what they do in the pre-start period — say from one week before the race until the boat is in the starting area.

The navigator's homework

The navigator's job doesn't stop mid-week; as soon as one race is over he starts preparing for the next.

Working from the race instructions (don't forget to send him a copy as soon as they arrive) he gathers together all his reference material such as charts, almanacs and tide tables. Then in the comfort of his armchair he can log:

- Details of local radio weather broadcasts.
- The expected tides for each leg of the race.
- The compass course from each buoy to the next.

Figure 2.1

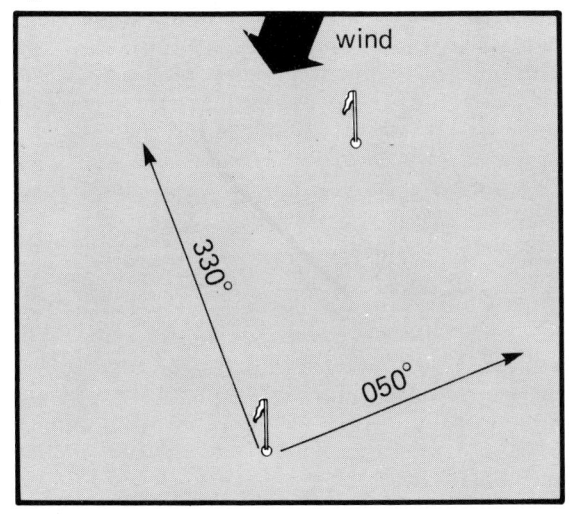

- For beating legs, the making tack bearings, e.g. "Tack if we're heading more than 050 degrees on port or less than 330 degrees on starboard" (figure 2.1).

If it is a serious race the navigator and helmsman need to get together a few days before to look at this data and make some dummy strategic decisions, e.g. "If we arrive at The Owers by 0200 we'll go inshore because the tide will still be running . . . ". By playing around like this you get a feel for the course and can work out a few basic rules for how you will sail the race. Believe me, it is much easier to do this now than at 0200 on a filthy night.

Two days before the race the navigator switches his attention to meteorology, making copies of the weather map each morning. Before going afloat he collects the most up-to-date weather chart available (either from your Weatherfax machine on board, from the marina's Weatherfax or by phone from a weather station).

It is vital to have an accurate weather map before you start because the picture won't change all that much in 36 hours. Updating an accurate chart at sea is much easier than starting from scratch and building one up from the shipping forecast. Armed with the current map and knowledge of how the systems have been moving for the past couple of days, the navigator is in the best possible position to advise on wind strategy.

The skipper's spadework

For an evening start it is as well to arrive at lunchtime and start making sure the boat is complete. Then if there is anything wrong you still have time to do something about it.

We have a permanent checklist on board which covers *everything* — from water to safety equipment

Before the race I like to check the mast myself.

— and I go through this with at least one helper, paying special attention to items that needed repairing after the last race. I also go up the mast myself before each outing to have a good look at the rig, paying particular attention to:
- The spreader roots (check for cracks).
- The sheaves.

The danger is that the Talurit ferrule on the halyard will be winched into the sheave, breaking its cheeks. Prevent this either by having a plastic ball on the halyard, or by using a small Talurit that will fit between the cheeks. For the main halyard, fit a slug to stop the Talurit going into the sheave at all.

By now the navigator and tactician have arrived and it is time for a little meeting to finalise strategy. Decisions are recorded in the navigator's notebook for future use.

The navigator has also prepared a little race pack for each crewman containing a map of the course, a list of buoys and a list of the crew members and their positions for the race. These are dished out as everyone comes on board and are a great way to make each person feel involved.

When everyone is assembled we usually have a get-together to make sure everyone has the right gear (but not too much of it) and knows where the lifejackets, harnesses, flares and other safety equipment are stowed.

Which sails to take?

A racing yacht can accumulate an enormous sail wardrobe. Needless to say they are not all taken to sea on every race — not least because the rating certificate limits the number that can be carried. For the current 'Yeoman' we probably have 40 sails, of which 20 will be stowed in the dockside shed ready for use. The choice is agonising. In our case we have to select 14 sails; this might be done as follows.

Look first at the weather forecast and decide if the wind is going to be light, medium or heavy.

Spinnakers are the first area of choice because so few can be taken (in our case, five). For offshore work *always* choose the heaviest (in case it blows up) plus a selection according to the expected windstrength. Inshore, go for the lighter kites in light winds and a range of heavies if it is blowing.

Inshore you only need one *main*, but choose the battens according to windstrength (the light, medium or heavy set). Offshore *always* use the heavy battens and *sew* them in (or they will fly out when you reef). If it is going to be really rough, consider taking a spare main.

Genoas come next. The range is Norcon; light/medium/heavy/number one; number two; number three. Choose a spread, but use windstrength to decide what to leave behind. If it is light we might do without the heavy number one, if it is heavy the Norcon would stay in the shed. If it is really blowing and we are racing inshore we might take two number three's, because there will be no time to repair damaged sails at sea.

You will also need a blooper and a staysail (these

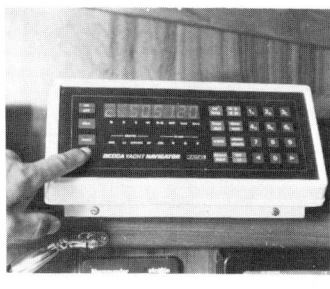

'Man Overboard' drill. Throw in an object such as a fender, record the latitude and longitude and detail one crew member to watch the 'man'. Start the engine, tack, and use a loop of rope for retrieval.

used to be very specialised but are far more multipurpose now, so you can get away with one).

Countdown to an offshore start

Now we are afloat at last, heading out to the start.

The first thing to do is . . . start eating! There won't be time after the start; indeed this meal will have to last all night. So let everyone tuck in while the pressure is off.

Then begin to gear people up to the idea that this is an offshore race by carrying out the 'man overboard' drill (chuck a fender over the side and time its recovery). I recommend:

1 The helmsman throws the fender and shouts "man overboard".
2 The navigator immediately pushes the 'lat/long' button on the Decca to record the boat's position.
3 All hands are called on deck (except the navigator).
4 One person is detailed to watch the fender.
5 Gybe or tack depending on which sails are set. If in doubt go head to wind — even if you have the kite up this will at least stop the boat.
6 Take down the spinnaker (if set) and sail or motor back.
7 Retrieve the fender from the leeward rail, sheeting in the main if necessary to heel the boat. Note that if this was for real you would tie a loop in the end of a rope so the man could put his foot in the loop and be winched aboard.

3 · During the race

During the race much of the skipper's time is taken up with strategy and boatspeed (which are fully covered in Part 2). But superb strategy is useless if the crew are disorganised, seasick or fall over the side, so in this and the next chapter I want to concentrate on the other part of the skipper's job — crew organisation and safety.

Decision-making afloat

Inshore we work on the principle of a tactical group. The navigator sorts out the tides, distance to the next mark and so forth while the tactician watches the other boats and checks wind direction. This frees the helmsman to concentrate on getting the best speed from the boat, although final decisions (say to tack, peel or gybe) are made by him. In short the helmsman steers, the tactician whispers in his ear and the navigator whispers in *his* ear.

Offshore things happen slower and you have to look further ahead. I often hand the wheel over to someone while I go below and chat to the navigator. Each time there is a change in wind or tide you need to rework your strategy:

"Our speed's increasing so we'll be at the headland well before the tide turns. We'd better keep on this tack and go in as close as possible."

"There's a low coming through — we'd better stand further out to benefit from the veer."

"If we stay on this tack we'll be off the beach at about 2100 and should get the land breeze. That'll lift us in to the mark — OK, we'll carry on like this."

"The wind's dropping. Let's tack now and keep up-tide of the mark — we don't want to be swept down and have to punch the tide all the way in."

The first few hours

The approach to the first few hours of any race is the same — put in maximum effort to try to take the lead. If you manage it, you will buoy up the crew's spirits and their ability level will stay high for most of the race. But a poor start gets everyone down, and you will have to work hard to cheer people up before they settle into the night's routine.

Watch systems

On a long ocean race conventional watch-keeping works best, but on the sort of short races we do (between 12 hours and 6 days) we find that a pairing system gives better results. Indeed, if you study another

LEFT *Chris Preston, the boat's organiser and deputy helmsman, at work on 'Yeoman'.* OPPOSITE *It is easy to hype the crew when other boats are close, but the test of a good skipper is to keep everyone alert offshore, particularly at night.*

boat closely you can often tell when she changes watch because she will slow down (a combination of the new crew taking time to get the feel of the boat, and their natural inclination to re-tune the boat immediately).

With our system the boatspeed stays pretty constant. It works like this:
- The navigator is unpaired, although someone is detailed as his helper.
- The rest of the crew are paired off. One member of each pair is on deck, the other is off watch.
- At any time a crewman can swap with his mate — so people are coming and going all the time. By and large most people swap every four hours, but if someone is tired or cold he might change after a couple of hours.
- For all manoeuvres (other than the most simple) everyone except the navigator is called up. Nothing leads to trouble more quickly than trying to work the boat shorthanded.
- The pair have one bunk allocated to them. The off-watch man either sleeps below or sits on the rail (where his weight does most good).
- If the crew are likely to be called up suddenly they forget about sleeping bags and sleep in oilskins.

The navigator organises his time around weather forecasts, ETA at buoys, and mealtimes. He has a sophisticated system of buzzers so he can catnap at his chart table and still wake at the right moment. For example, he might
    plot his current position
    plot forward three hours
    ask to be woken if there is any change, then catnap
    wake for the midnight weather forecast
    plot forward three hours
    catnap again
    wake for the run-in to the mark
    catch the early-morning weather forecast
    have breakfast
    catnap again.

Seasickness

I count myself lucky not to be bothered by seasickness because I've seen how much suffering it causes. There seem to be several types of victim:
- People with inherent problems of the middle ear. They will always be seasick on short passages, so the solution is to stick to long voyages and give up short-distance ocean racing.
- People suffering from nerves. Essentially the situation is so worrying for them (big seas, dangerous manoeuvres) that fear makes them sick. They need more experience inshore before venturing out to sea.
- People who haven't prepared themselves properly. Lack of sleep, too much alcohol, rich food, cold and lack of liquid are all contributory factors which can be removed with a bit of forward planning.

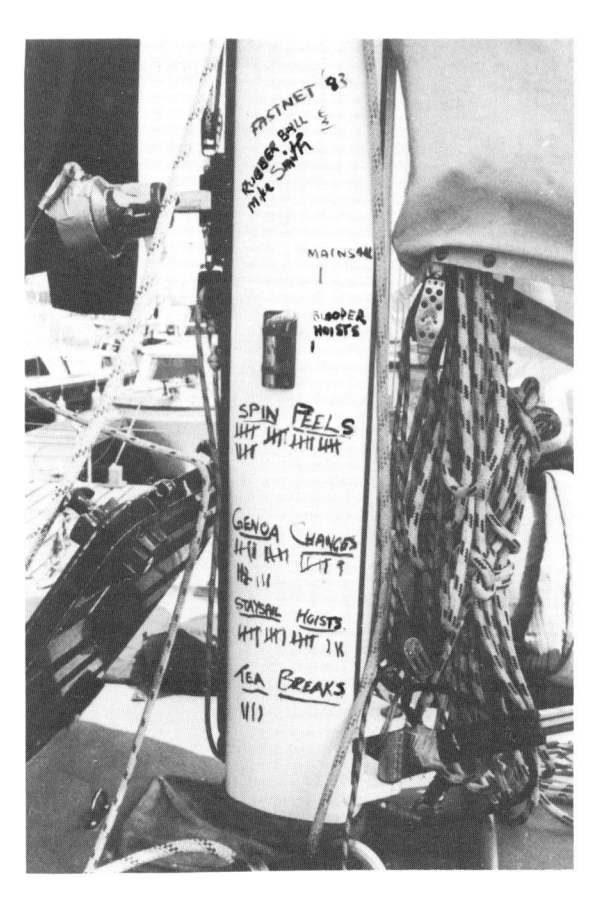

Here is some advice for those in distress.

Take plenty of fresh air (unless it is very cold).

If on deck, scan the horizon. Alternatively, go below and lie down.

Try pills if you like, but remember they may make you drowsy. Those which you tape behind the ear (and dissolve through the skin straight to the middle ear) seem to work well.

As skipper all you can do is make sure the boat is properly ventilated; a system where air enters through vents in the hatches and exits through a hole in the wheel trough is ideal. A sump tray to catch leakage from the engine will help prevent that delicious aroma of diesel from the bilges.

Pacing

New crewmen tend to be over-enthusiastic early in a race but keep nothing in reserve for the closing stages, in contrast to the old hand who has learned to pace himself. So calm the crew down, and make them go below when they have done their bit.

Eye masks (and even ear plugs) can make sleeping easier, though in reality you're unlikely to do more than doze on a short race. Have a warm drink and a chocolate bar to help wake yourself up and, conversely, don't pile into the coffee before trying to go to sleep.

On a more basic note, *don't* let people pee over the side (that's when they can fall off, especially at night). Get them to use a bucket in the cockpit (or even the cockpit drain hole). For more serious business they will have to wait until the boat is on an even keel, because the heads don't function when the boat is heeling.

LEFT *A record of the foredeck's activity on 'Yeoman' during the Fastnet.*

DURING THE RACE

RIGHT *It is important to have someone on board who can raise morale: Alistair 'Rubber Ball' Munroe fulfills this role admirably on 'Yeoman'.*

Morale

In selecting the crew make sure you have someone who can raise morale when things have gone wrong. The skipper is usually not the best person to do this (he often feels he has let the crew down) and, indeed, the skipper and navigator may be at loggerheads in trying to sort out the mess and need a cheery person to step between them. In short, the hyped-up people you need to make the boat go may overreact without a foil, and it is the skipper's job to make sure there is someone on board to fit that bill.

Going aground

Nothing is worse for morale than hitting the bottom. If you are *beating*, tack immediately, then pin in all the sails (to make her heel) and reach off. If this fails move all the crew to the bow (which lifts the keel tremendously) and try to gybe round. Finally, try putting up the kite to drag her sideways.

If you are *running*, luff or gybe immediately; but if the boat stops, drop the spinnaker, hoist a genoa and try to beat off.

4 · Survival conditions

As the wind increases there comes a point where to carry on in racing mode will endanger the boat and crew. The skipper now needs to make a conscious decision to begin survival procedure, and to tell everyone that this is the case. It doesn't necessarily mean that the race is over (the storm may pass), but for the next few hours the main objective is just to hang on.

This is not a book about heavy weather, but a few points won't go amiss. As skipper, make sure that
- Everyone has on a harness and an inflated lifejacket.
- In each oilskin pocket there is a flare pack, whistle and torch. (These are issued to each crew member before the race starts).
- The storm jib and trysail are set. (Note it is vital to have practised this at the dockside in calm conditions).
- There are four sheets on the jib (two on each side).
- There are only two or three people on deck (this minimises the chance of someone being swept overboard if the boat is rolled over).
- Everyone down below has oilskins on, is alert to possible problems, and is sitting on the cabin sole (*not* on the bunks) to improve stability.
- The cooker is off. Food — and for that matter sleep — are not your main worries, since most storms are relatively short-lived. As an example, we were *becalmed* 4 hours before and 12 hours after the 1979 Fastnet storm.
- Someone on deck keeps a constant watch on the mast and forestay.
- People coming on deck hook on *before* they step out into the cockpit.
- No one is hooked on to the lifelines — they must use the jackstays or something more solid.

Should you run, reach or beat?

Running downhill in big waves is highly dangerous in a modern boat. You have little control over the boat's speed which simply depends on the steepness of the wave; careering down a wave at 20 knots is terrifying enough, but your problems will really start when you hit the trough ahead.

Bear in mind too that modern designs are very buoyant aft, so an overtaking wave tends to pick up the stern and pitchpole the boat. Finally, running takes you towards lee shores, the main source of danger in a storm.

These problems are removed by turning the boat onto a close reach — say 45 degrees to 55 degrees off the wind — which is the course I recommend. Let the main and jib well out so that if a wave makes the boat round up the sails flap early, giving you time to pull her off before she tacks.

The main objective is to avoid breakers, so steer up each wave to miss the worst of the crest. At the top have a good look ahead to spot the real monsters coming — then luff or bear away to get out of their path.

The final plus for the close reach is that if you have to alter course, tacking is safer than gybing.

Extreme conditions

If the wind increases further you may have to lie a-hull (i.e. stop). This needs to be done carefully because modern boats tend to lie broadside-on to the wind, with the danger of a knockdown. I prefer to set up drogues (sailbags tied to long lines securely attached to the mast) and lie bows-on, because the lack of buoyancy in the bow minimises the pitching caused by each wave.

Action to take in various disasters
Broken mast. Either cut the mast away or strap the pieces onto the boat (the main danger is that the sharp ends will punch a hole in the hull). Then lie a-hull, and motor (or sail) home when conditions ease up.

Holed. If the hole is caused by a fitting pulling out, ram in a softwood plug.

For a larger hole in the hull, stuff sleeping bags or mattresses into it and lash a floorboard on top to hold them in place. Begin the Mayday procedure.

When to abandon ship
I was in Falmouth when some of the abandoned boats were towed in after the 1979 Fastnet. Looking inside it was clear why the crews had left — the yachts appeared to be complete write-offs. However, there they were, still afloat and capable of supporting the crew, many of whom, sadly, had taken to liferafts and later drowned.

The moral is clear: only abandon when you are *sure* the boat is going down. Then
- Have everyone on deck.
- Make sure their lifejackets are inflated and they are wearing plenty of clothes.
- Detail someone to bring the flare box, torches, water, food and a knife.
- Launch the liferaft late (otherwise a wave may rip it away from the boat before you have a chance to board it).
- Each person hooks on to the umbilical cord and slides down it, hooking on to the liferaft as soon as he's aboard.

Rendering assistance
If you see or hear a problem, enter the time in your log and immediately go to help. You will be given a generous time allowance for doing so.
- Call all the crew on deck.
- Start the motor.
- Have heaving lines ready.
- If you need to transfer people off the other boat launch your liferaft and tow people across in that.

You may have rescued the other crew, but hypothermia can still kill them. Take them down below and wrap them in blankets. (A foil blanket from the Red Cross kit is ideal). One member of the crew should have been on a first-aid course and be ready to sew up wounds and treat other injuries.

5 · Starting to windward

In this chapter I want to look at the way to approach a beating start. This involves making a plan (deciding which side of the beat is favoured and where on the line to start) and then carrying out that plan in the midst of the other boats.

Usually it is the other boats that are the problem — particularly when you are racing in a mixed fleet. The last thing you want is to make a perfect start, only to find there is a monster to windward who chomps slowly through your weather. So I will touch on mixed-fleet strategy, and also add a few thoughts on those inevitable occasions when your start goes wrong.

Planning the start

Your start plan begins to take shape as soon as you leave the dock, because that is the time to begin monitoring the wind and tide.

Tide. Dig out your tidal charts and look up the currents expected over the racecourse for the next few hours. Then check the wind direction, and try to guess which courses might be set. Armed with this information you are ready to do some dummy tactical runs:

"With the wind in this direction they'll probably send us to buoy A. The tide will turn first on the north shore, so we'll want to keep left on the beat to catch the first of the flood."

"Yes, but at low tide we'll never get over this bank, so we'd do best to head for the main channel and tack down it."

"OK, if we get a course like that we'll go left into the main channel and tack when we can lay the mark."

"Now, what if they send us to B . . ."

If you have thought out the problems in this way, when the real course is set you will be able to make your plan quickly, then concentrate on where to start and how to out-manoeuvre the other boats.

Wind. As soon as you are clear of the land the navigator starts his stopwatch and begins to plot wind direction against time; he will carry on doing this until the race is over. Alternatively, the boat's computer can do this automatically. This is the only way to come to a sensible conclusion about what the wind is doing; in figure 5.1, for example, the wind is oscillating *and* gradually veering, which suggests you should go right on the beat.

Our navigator gets the wind readings from his instruments, but if you don't have a true wind read-out

Figure 5.1

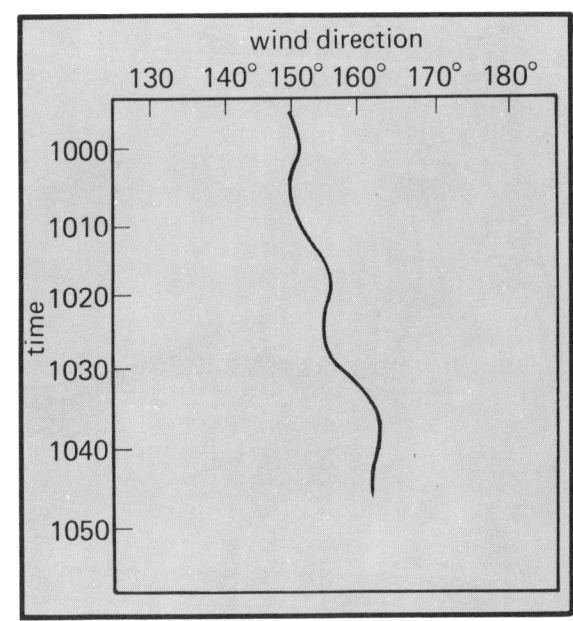

Starting to windward: it is vital to be in the front rank to keep your wind clear.

simply point the boat head-to-wind occasionally and read the compass. You should do this in any case when you are near the line to make sure the instruments are working.

Sussing out the line

As soon as the line is laid, sail down it and take a bearing (using a hand-bearing compass). Let's say the line bears 240 degrees and the navigator gives the mean wind direction as 160 degrees. Evaluate the line as follows.

1. Add 90 degrees to the mean wind direction.
   160 degrees + 90 degrees = 250 degrees
   A square line would bear 250 degrees.
2. Our line bears 240 degrees. This is less than 250 degrees so the starboard end is favoured.
3. If the line bearing was more than 250 degrees, the port end would be best.

This is summed up in figure 5.2. (In fact, if the wind goes on veering as predicted in figure 5.1, the starboard end will be even more favoured by the time we start.)

Figure 5.2

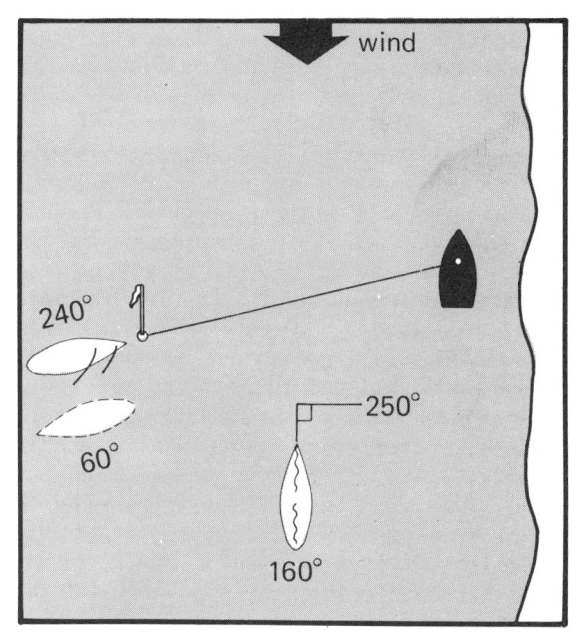

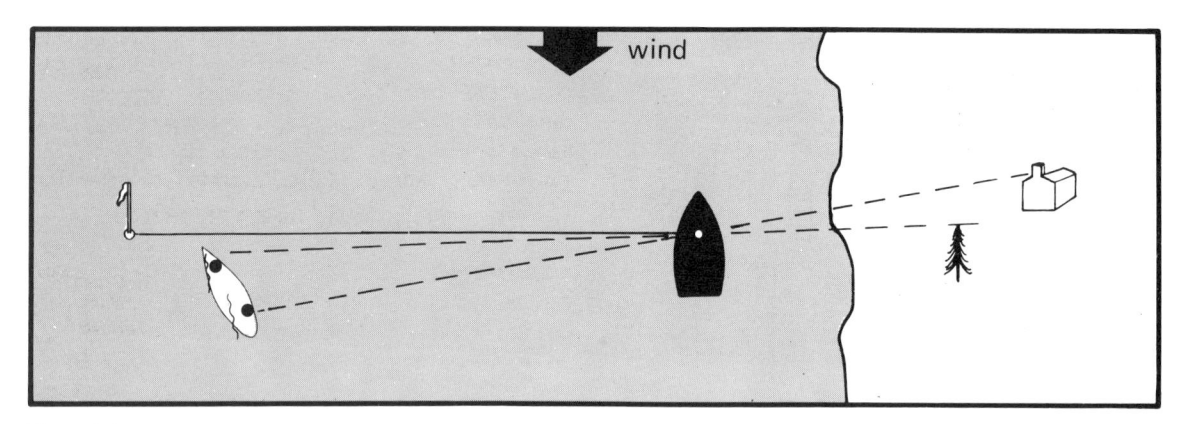

Figure 5.3

Lastly, convert the line bearing into a back bearing for use later.

240 degrees − 180 degrees = 60 degrees

Taking transits. When the starting gun is about to fire you will need to know how far you are from the line. Sitting at the stern of a 40-foot boat doesn't make this any easier, because it is the *bow* that has to be behind the line at the gun, not the helmsman. There are two solutions to this problem: choose a good bowman and take a transit on the line.

Your bowman must be someone you have worked with before and who understands your system. He will need a hand-bearing compass (tied to the forestay) and a stopwatch. Sail up to the pin and when the bowman judges the bow to be 'on', you both take a transit through the mast of the committee boat. In figure 5.3 the bowman's transit is a tree on the shore, whereas yours is a house. (If there is no shore behind the committee boat you can try sailing up to it and taking transits the other way, through the pin.)

When you come to start for real you can edge forwards until that house lines up with the committee boat's mast again, when you'll know you are on the line. The bowman is watching his transit, too, and giving his view on how far back you are: five fingers for five boat lengths, four fingers for four lengths and so on.

If the committee boat is hidden behind sails at the start your preparation will come into its own. If the bowman can still see the tree ashore he can take bearings on it and guide you forwards until the tree bears 240 degrees. Alternatively he may be able to take bearings on the pin and edge you up until it bears 60 degrees.

If there is a bulge in the line, forget about transits and push forwards until you are in the front rank. There will either be a general recall or the OOD will let the fleet go; in either event you must be up there with the opposition.

Making a good mid-line start

Ten minutes to go. Keep close to the committee boat so everyone can start their watches accurately on the ten-minute gun. When the course goes up the navigator draws it out on a plastic chart which is then firmly taped to a convenient part of the cockpit. Jog carefully along on starboard, make your plan and let everyone know it: "I'd like to start at the starboard end and hold that tack to get out into the stronger tide".

The navigator continues to check the wind and you may need to modify your plan accordingly: "It's veered even more — 170 degrees now — it's well biased to the starboard end"."OK, there's obviously going to be

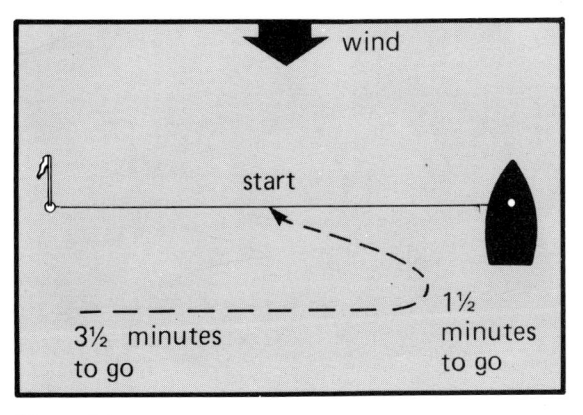

Figure 5.4

a pile-up there — we'll start further along to avoid the crush".

Look at the windspeed and choose the better genoa of the two on deck. Hoist it, come on the wind (with everyone in position on the weather rail) and make sure the sail is properly set up. By now the bowman is in position calling the other boats (with the genoa up you can't see anything to leeward).

Next reach down the line to find how long it takes to sail from one end to the other (suppose this is two minutes). It may take up to a third longer at the start because of windshadows. Your plan is to start in the middle of the line: what you need to do now is work out how you are going to get there. Bear in mind that:

- You want to be on starboard for as short a time as possible (you are much more manoeuvrable on port).
- It will take about one minute to build up speed on starboard.

We decide to set off on port from the pin three and half minutes before the gun, tack with one and a half minutes to go, then reach back the other way to start in the middle of the line (figure 5.4).

We now have a plan and a method of achieving it — the next five minutes will show if we were right.

Five minutes to go. We check our stopwatches (it is the five-minute gun that counts, not the ten) and make sure there is no change of course. Then I take a deep breath and begin to work our way towards the pin as planned. With three and a half minutes to go we set off on port towards the committee boat, sailing about three lengths below the line and watching the starboard tackers carefully. I want to tack with a minute and a half to go and luckily there seems to be a clear area — round we go. At this moment the bowman spots a large yacht reaching fast from behind the committee boat, and I stay head to wind to encourage her to pass behind us and on down the line. We complete our tack and start developing speed on the reach. I'm sailing about two lengths from the line to give myself room to harden up well before the gun (the act of rounding up will slow us down and also start us drifting sideways towards any boat to leeward).

But my plan is going wrong — there is someone ahead and, as overtaking boat, we can't sail straight into her transom! She is about the same size as us and I decide to slow down to try to open up a gap between us. This seems to work well, and is also bunching the boats to weather, which may stop them driving over us.

The boat ahead bears off to start her run at the line and we follow suit, rounding onto the wind with 15

BELOW *A hand-bearing compass is used at the start to take a bearing on the committee boat (or pin).*

STARTING TO WINDWARD

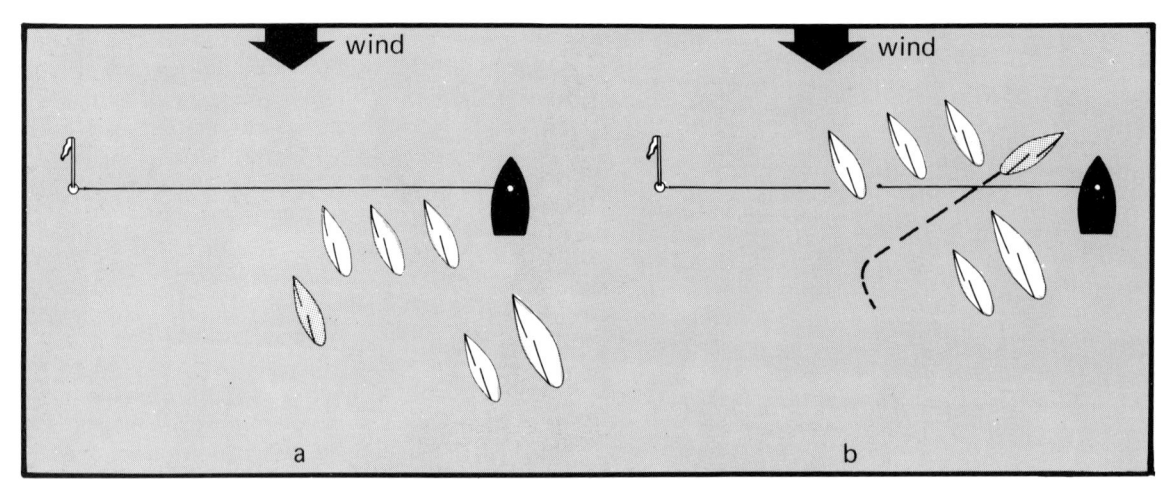

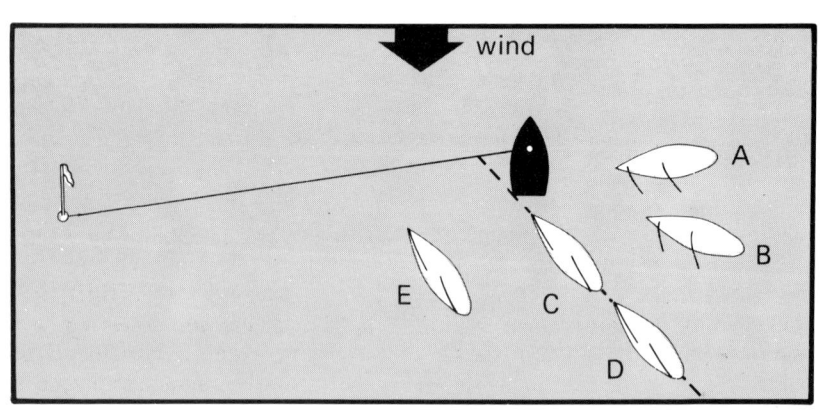

Figure 5.5

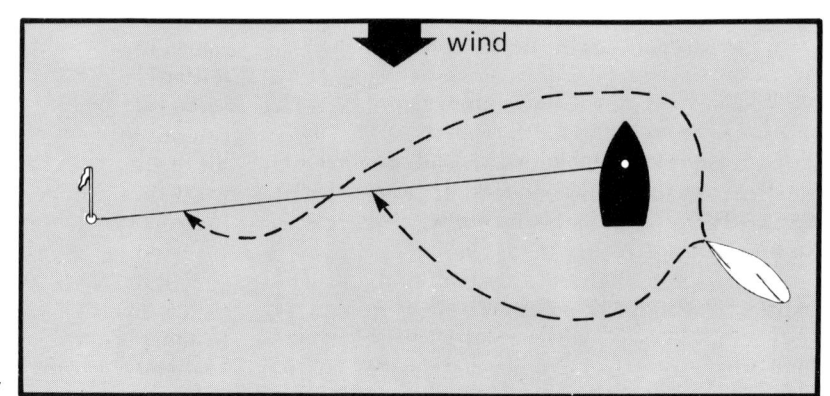

Figure 5.6

Figure 5.7

34

This start has gone badly wrong for 10300 and 2546. They need to take prompt remedial action, tacking or bearing away to gain clear air.

seconds to go. We cross the line just after the gun all right but without full speed — that slowing manoeuvre cost us. Luckily the boats on either side aren't going too well either, and as our boatspeed comes up we inch ahead into clear air and safety. Now for some fast sailing . . .

At the start

On this occasion we got away cleanly from the start line, but all too often things go wrong. If you have made a blunder try to rectify it immediately: some of the boats to weather will still be going slowly (figure 5.5) and you may be able to tack and cross them. If you leave it a while they will pick up speed and, especially if they are bigger boats, you will be penned in for ever.

Making a starboard-end start

If the line is biased to starboard there is likely to be a number of boats (A, B in figure 5.6) fanning in from above the committee boat. Of course they have no rights over boats starting properly (like C), but that doesn't stop them trying!

If you want to stay out of trouble start a little way down the line using the techniques suggested for a mid-line start. Alternatively come in late (like D) on the lay line to the committee boat and tack as soon as you're clear of the line.

But if you *do* decide to try for the pole position, come in on port until you cross the lay line to the committee boat. Tack just past the lay line with about 45 seconds to go (like C). You are now close-hauled and can sail slowly forwards, adjusting your speed so you hit the line with the gun. Meanwhile you can have a great time calling A and B up, and boats to leeward (E) can't trouble you because you are already hard on the wind.

If things go wrong and you get trapped in coffin corner like B, either gybe immediately (figure 5.7) or (if there is time) sail to windward of the committee boat and reach along the line, dipping into a hole just before the gun.

STARTING TO WINDWARD

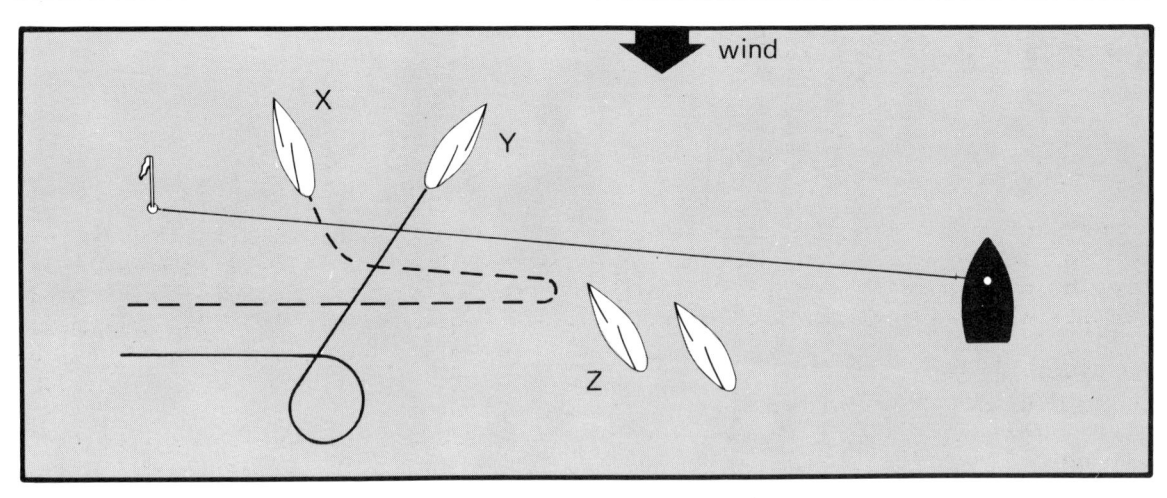

Figure 5.8

Making a port-end start

If the pin end is favoured aim to be sailing by it on port with about two minutes to go (figure 5.8). Have a look at the rest of the fleet — if they are well back you can risk gybing round and making a port-tack start (like Y). On the rare occasions when this pays off you get a marvellous boost as you cross the whole fleet and out into clear air.

But if the other boats are lining up properly continue on port (like X) until you reach the first one (Z). If you think she's late, tack ahead of her and reach back so you start by the pin. If you reckon she is early, duck underneath her and tack into the nearest hole. Then control your speed to make a gap to leeward, and reach towards the pin.

Above all, don't be in the second row: this is not only slow, but with your wind cut off you may not be able to clear the pin. If you look like being a second ranker, gybe round quickly and either cross the line on port or tack onto starboard in a hole.

Starting in mixed fleets

The golden rule when starting with boats of different sizes is *make sure the boats to weather are your size or smaller*. If you start to leeward of a dinosaur she will either drive over the top of you or, if she is badly sailed, pin you down and stop you tacking on windshifts.

To avoid this come in on port as usual but be very careful about where you tack onto starboard. Have a good look at the boats approaching — if they are little boats with big ones behind tack ahead of them all, but if there is a crowd of large boats with little ones behind duck the big ones and tack amongst the small fry.

If you find yourself surrounded by big boats try to work into a position where you can tack after the gun — starting late by the committee boat would do the trick. If all else fails you might be able to force a general recall by pushing over the line early — the monsters to windward will usually follow suit and the OOD may bring everyone back to try again.

If you are sailing one of the large boats it is much easier to recover from a bad start. If you start well in a big boat you're sure to pull out into clear air, but even if you botch it you have the speed to screw over the top of a little boat or bear away through her lee. Size may not cure all ills, but it certainly helps at the start.

6 · Starting offwind

Offwind starts are common in yacht racing, particularly if you are going offshore. This is where many ex-dinghy helmsmen come unstuck, because most of their starts will have been to windward.

A touch of theory

The polar chart shows that for each windstrength there is one wind angle that gives the best boatspeed on a reach.

In figure 6.1, derived from the polar table on pages 18-19, the 12-knot windspeed curve shows that the fastest boatspeed is achieved at a wind angle of 110 degrees true. As the wind becomes lighter the fastest course is closer to the wind (at a windspeed of 5 knots the best wind angle is 90 degrees true). In stronger breezes you go best with wind well aft (at a windspeed of 20 knots the optimal wind angle is 140 degrees true).

All well and good, you may say, but what's that got to do with offwind starts? The answer is simple: just after the start you must be sailing at your maximum boatspeed in order to break clear of the boats around. So in light winds try to set off at about 90 degrees to the true wind, in 20 knots hammer off at about 140 degrees and so on.

Maximising boatspeed is the most important objective at the start. Before looking at how to achieve this, here are some other important requirements to bear in mind.

- Don't start underneath anyone.
- Don't start at the windward end of the line (you'll be luffed out).
- Don't start in a bunch.
- Don't come in at an angle to the line if this will encourage the boat to leeward to luff.

Figure 6.1

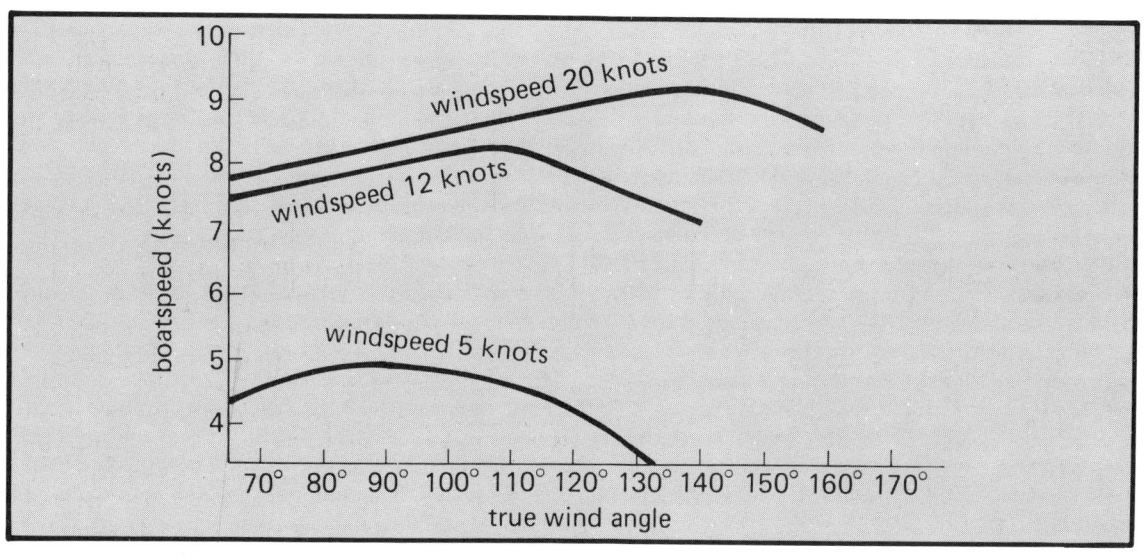

STARTING OFFWIND

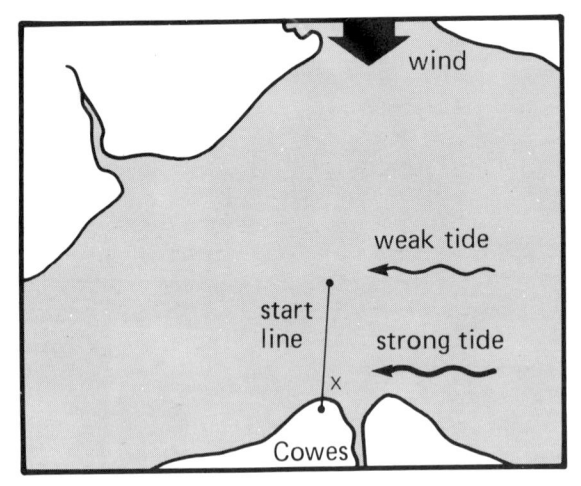

Figure 6.2

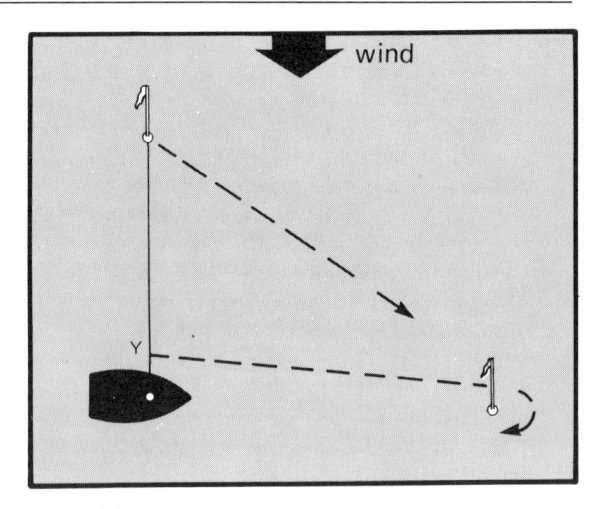

Figure 6.3

- Don't start at less than your maximum speed (or the boats to weather will roll over the top of you).
- Don't break out the spinnaker before the gun unless you are certain to be late.

Preparing for the start

First, use a current stick or tidal atlas to see if there is a tide gradient along the startline. Figure 6.2 shows a common situation for the start of the Fastnet, the boats starting at X having the advantage.

Next check with the navigator that the line is not biased in relation to the first mark. Figure 6.3 shows a ludicrous (but common) situation where the course is so angled that there's only one place to start (Y), because this gives the shortest distance to the buoy.

Let's suppose, though, that there are no funny effects and you can start anywhere on the line. By and large the best way to handle a reaching start is by means of a timed run, because this gives you the confidence to head for the line at full speed. To achieve this:

1. Position the boat on the line so the bowman can take a bearing on the pin (or committee boat) *and* on an object ashore (in case the pin is obscured at the start).

2. Now choose a point about 60 seconds' sailing from the line, and try a couple of dummy runs. Suppose you find it takes 65 seconds to sail from your marker to the line: when you start for real you will want to set off with about 80 seconds to go because of the blanketing effect of boats to windward.

3. A lobster-pot float makes an ideal marker, but if no fixed floating object is available you may be able to take a transit between two objects on shore. This can be very handy when the transit is parallel to the line (figure 6.4) because you keep flexibility; you can start from A, B or C (to avoid bunches of boats) and go for the line knowing your timing will be spot on. If no transit is available you will have to make do with the bearing of an object on shore.

Starting on a beam reach or close reach

Now all the variables are sorted out and there are only a few minutes left to the gun. The navigator is watching out for bunches: "There'll be a big pile-up at the pin; there's a clear spot in the middle of the line – let's get down." So we line up on our marker and reach for the mid-point of the line. A bigger boat has the same idea and for a moment it looks as though she is going to sail over us, so we

STARTING OFFWIND

screw up and she bears away through our lee. Great – we can catch a tow on her wake and really motor down the first leg.

As the seconds tick away the bowman is taking bearings on the pin. "Half a minute to go – you're too early." We luff to avoid being over, then bear away to cross the line with full speed. The navigator is down below with the radio: "We're OK – G25 and KA806 were recalled. Let's go."

And so we're away, nicely positioned with a gap to windward and a wave to ride. If only it were always like that! The main problem, of course, is the other boats, so here are a few thoughts on outwitting them at the start.

- If your boat is large you *must* pick a clear spot or risk towing a bunch of smaller fry.
- If your boat is small line up with someone larger but watch out for her windshadow.
- Never go too far from the line – if something happens (such as the wind dropping) you won't make it back by the gun.
- Make your final approach to the line on the fastest point of sailing (as described earlier). If you come in closer to the wind people will luff you. If you come in freer you will lose speed. After the gun try to stay on the fastest point of sailing.
- If someone below starts luffing, play cat-and-mouse with her – keep close, then duck underneath her transom as she puts in a more violent luff.
- If you are too early, luff to lengthen your course to the line. You may also pick up a little speed, which will be useful when you bear away after the gun. But if there is a bunch to windward all you can do is bear away early; this prevents your being over but leaves you going slowly at the start.
- If you are too late there is nothing you can do! You will probably finish up with a large bunch to windward, neatly cutting off your power supply. You then have two choices. Either luff sharply through a gap into clear air. Alternatively, if the bunch is a long way to weather and the boats are luffing each other, sail

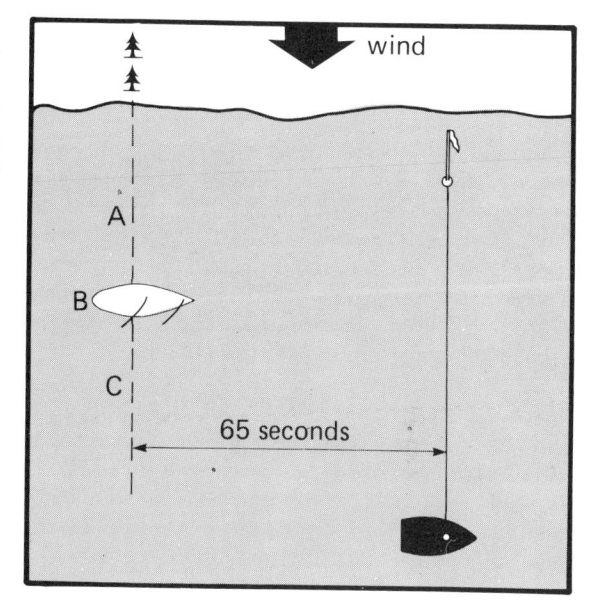

Figure 6.4

straight on and wait for the gap to open. *Never* bear away below the fastest course, because your boatspeed will drop dramatically (5 degrees may lose you 0.5 knot) and a string of boats will sail over you, one after the other.

Starting on a broad reach

This is much the same as the technique described earlier, except you will be setting a spinnaker.

- Don't set the spinnaker before the gun.
- When you set off from your marker for the line, make sure no one is below you. If there is a boat to leeward you will have to wait until she sets her spinnaker before you follow suit. If you set your kite first and she luffs you, you're dead!
- Set the pole with 1 minute to go.
- Hoist the spinnaker in stops 20 seconds before the gun and bang it out with 5 seconds to go.
- Bear away to help the kite fill and to make sure you don't broach.
- Where on the line you start is irrelevant provided you have clear air. Note that a leeward

39

STARTING OFFWIND

start often pays because you can pick up speed after the gun by luffing, and this is particularly true in light winds when the speed differential is great.

Many people fear starting to leeward on a broad reach because of the windshadows of the boats to weather. This is not too great a problem, however, because your boatspeed soon pulls the apparent wind ahead. A true wind at 135 degrees, for example, becomes an apparent wind of 85 degrees when the boat is up to 7 knots (figure 6.5) which means the windshadows are angled *back* from the line.

Starting on a run

Starting on a run poses special problems because the windshadow from the slower boats is large and traps the leaders. Prepare for the start as before but go for the line at the optimum wind angle (i.e. to make the best VMG downwind). Try to avoid being part of a bunch because you will then be locked in to their heading – which is usually too high. In figure 6.6, for example, D always tends to luff taking the whole group too high. E gybes onto port, has nothing to do with the group and sails at her own angle. When the bunch gybes E can gybe back and feed through them, still sailing her own course.

Don't set the blooper until you are clear of other boats, because you lose manoeuvrability with it up. Unless of course you are late for the start, in which case pile on all sail!

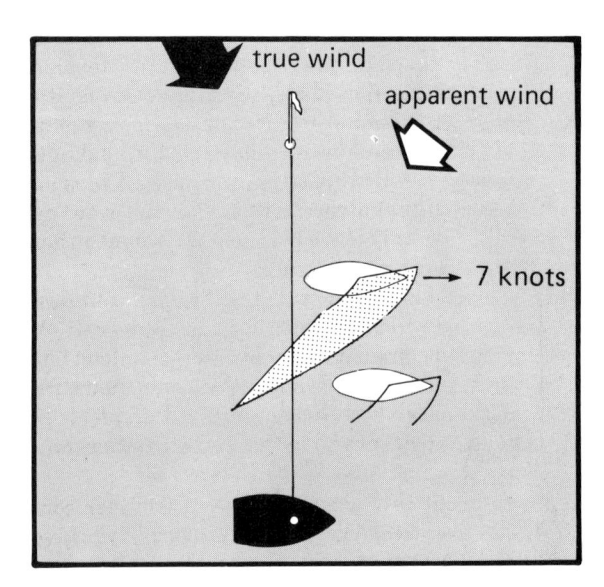

Figure 6.5

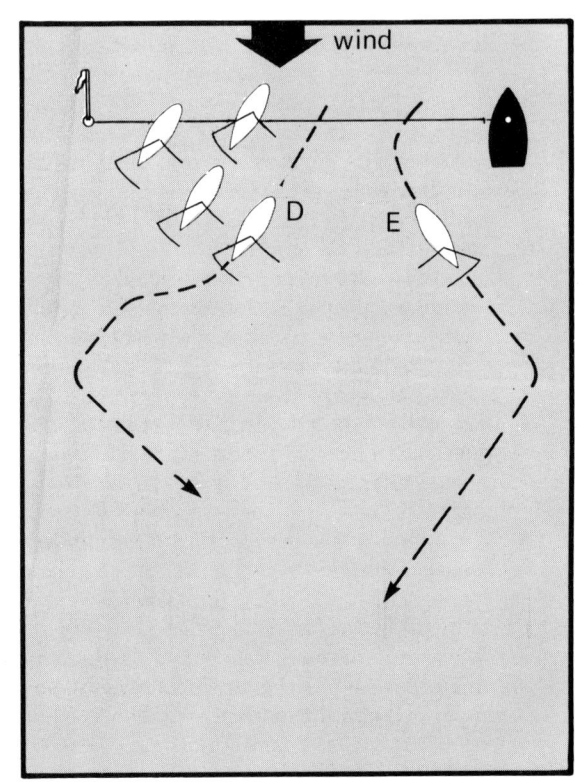

Figure 6.6

7 · Beating in medium winds

It is a marvellous feeling to power the boat to windward in 10 to 20 knots of wind, particularly if she is set up properly and the helmsman and trimmers are working together. To achieve this sort of harmony you need to know how to balance the boat and how to guide her gently but firmly up the beat; the sections below explain in some detail how to do this.

Setting up a masthead rig

Before you set the boat up check the expected windstrength with the navigator.

Rigging tension

You should only alter the rigging tension before the race if you have a mast ram (it is illegal to alter mast tension *during* the race except in emergencies).

If you have a ram and are sailing offshore, set up the rigging for heavy weather since you can never tell if the wind will increase later. If you are sailing inshore, guess the day's wind and set to what is expected.

If the boat doesn't have a ram leave the bottlescrews permanently set up for the worst conditions – fiddling with them is a sure way to de-tune the boat.

Sheet weights and lead positions

Choose the sheet diameter according to the wind strength. The positions of the lead blocks should have been determined in practice and painted on the deck.

Choice of genoa

Before the start, everyone has his or her own idea about which genoa to set. When the wittering has died down, narrow the choice to a couple of sails and bring both on deck, then hoist the most suitable one for the expected windspeed.

At this stage stay on one tack – with half the crew down below putting on oilskins there is a good chance of snagging the foresail as you go about, and nothing ruins a sail quicker.

If your first choice of genoa was wrong, change to the other sail and pack the old one immediately – packing on deck is slow and with the start approaching you don't want the foredeck knee-deep in Mylar.

Trimming the genoa

1. Pump up the backstay to its approximate position for the current conditions (I like to have a calibrated rod alongside the backstay to act as a gauge).
2. The genoa trimmer calls for the halyard tension to be adjusted. Note that increasing the tension moves the air flow forwards and removes the wrinkles just behind the forestay – as a rule of thumb those wrinkles should be *just* wound out. Most people sail with too much halyard tension and play the halyard excessively – even on 'Yeoman' we only move it 3 inches (7.5 mm) either way from the mean setting.
3. Now luff slowly and watch the genoa telltales. They should all break together; if the upper windward telltale breaks first move the sheet lead forwards. If the upper leeward or the lower windward telltale misbehaves first, move the lead aft. If in doubt, it is better to have the lead aft rather than forward.
4. As the boat goes up the beat the trimmer constantly calls for adjustment to the backstay to give the right amount of forestay sag. The genoa halyard may need to be altered in sympathy.

Note that the backstay tension is determined by the genoa trimmer and not by the main trimmer, who simply has to adjust his leech tension to suit. The backstay does more than anything to give the

BEATING IN MEDIUM WINDS

helmsman 'feel' – if it is too tight there will be only a narrow 'groove' where the boat has life, and she will be difficult to steer.

When you are happy with the genoa note the sheet position and align the lead on the other deck so the setting can be repeated on the other tack.

Genoa leech line. Few people adjust the leech line often enough. As the sheet is wound in the leech gets tighter, so slacken off the leech line until the leech is about to shiver. Conversely tighten the leech line as the sheet is slackened.

Setting the mainsail

Although you may later pull the mast into an exotic shape, begin by setting the runners and the backstay to give the mast an even bend. Check this by sighting the mast against the shrouds (which are straight). Some mainsails have fancy marks just behind the luff to help judge the bend, but really they are unnecessary.

If the boat is well sorted out a set of figures will give the runner and backstay positions required for the current genoa and windspeed. Remember that as the backstay comes on you will need to re-tension the genoa halyard.

Now trim the main to give a good feel on the helm. Begin with the boom on the centreline and ease the sheet until the telltales on the leech are all streaming. If you have more than 5 degrees of weather helm ease the traveller to leeward until you get 5 degrees. Now look at the front part of the main: if the sail is too full it will be backwinded by the genoa, so pull the bubble out by easing off the runners to give more mast bend until the backwinding *almost* disappears. If your boat has no runners you can achieve the same effect by pulling on the backstay or the cunningham.

All these adjustments make the leech ease off, so the traveller can come up to windward slightly to restore weather helm. But note that the boom only very rarely comes to weather of the centreline and then only in light airs. Before the start it is important to play around with all these controls – particularly the runners and backstay – until the helm feels right.

Flattener

The flattener does not reduce sail area significantly – it is used in medium winds to control the curve in the bottom of the mainsail (mast bend controls curve in

'Fast stripes' on the genoa (LEFT, TOP) help the trimmer gauge the chord of the sail. Stripes on the crosstrees would help judge the leech position. The leech of the genoa should be parallel to the main (OPPOSITE) to give a good slot. LEFT To trim the main, watch the leech telltales, the 'Fast stripes' and the 'bubble' at the luff (which indicates mast bend).

BEATING IN MEDIUM WINDS

the middle of the sail). To depower the main gradually pull on the flattener, and then tension the cunningham carefully to even out the curve over the whole height of the sail.

Using the flattener in this way allows the mainsail to be cut very full in the foot (which is good for light winds) and it is so useful that it is hydraulically controlled on our boat.

Vang
Only put on sufficient vang tension to allow the mainsheet trimmer to move the traveller without difficulty. Don't forget to let it off before you bear away.

The slot
On 'Yeoman XXIII' we had an excellent 'toast-rack' arrangement for moving the genoa lead in any direction. If your boat lacks this, always sail with the barber-hauler rigged so that when you ease the main in a gust you can haul the genoa lead to leeward. (If you leave the genoa pinned in, the slot will close as the main goes down and the main will be backwinded.) The barber-hauler should be rigged with a hook so you can detach it before you tack – never tack with it on.

Above all, you need lines painted on the deck so you can align the genoa (and hence the slot) immediately on the other tack.

Babystay
To prevent the mast waggling around, tension the babystay (it pulls 'against' the runners). This is also a method of inducing mast bend.

Final checks
Now settle down and sail fast, checking your boatspeed (not VMG) against the performance chart. If we are going slowly, I generally:
1 Adjust the runners first to alter the chord of the main. This can give a tremendous increase in

boatspeed, even when the rig previously looked right.
2 Alter the genoa halyard next. If the wind has dropped it will usually be too tight; if the wind is rising it will usually be too loose.
3 Alter the inboard/outboard setting of the genoa lead (e.g. move it inboard if the wind is dropping).

Lastly, look at what the other boats are doing. If you have the number one up but they are all flying number threes, try to work out why. If you can't, sail over to one of them, wish the helmsman good morning and slip your query into the ensuing banter.

Setting up a fractional rig

Most of the principles outlined above apply equally well to a fractional rig. The main differences are:
1 The backstay trims the curve in the mainsail (on a masthead rig the backstay tightens the forestay).
2 The runners adjust the tension in the forestay.
3 The vang is used more to windward, when you want to bend the mast without slackening the leech too much.

Trim

The boat won't go well unless she is trimmed properly. Firstly check that everyone is trying – the crew on the rail have their boots over the side and no one is sleeping in the leeward bunks.

If possible, the genoa sheet should be taken around the leeward winch and across to one on the weather side so the trimmer can play it from the windward deck, where his weight is most use. This also keeps the trimmer out of the slot and clear of flying spray.

It is hard to keep everyone keyed up like this offshore, but it does pay dividends.

LEFT *The effect of the barber-hauler is to move the genoa clew outboard. Do this when overpowered (you can then carry the same headsail in a few more knots of wind) or when the main is eased (to keep the slot open). Note also how the positions of the lead blocks are numbered so the settings can be recorded. Calibration is vital to good tuning.*

Check heel by using an inclinometer – essentially a jumped-up spirit level. Offshore, it pays to ease the traveller down and move the genoa lead outboard and sail the boat more upright; in 'Yeoman' we aim for 20 to 24 degrees of heel, although every boat is different. This is because leeway is critical on long offshore legs – if you don't believe me just watch the Decca and see how the 'course made good' slips.

Inshore, leeway seems to be less critical and the ability to screw up close to the wind takes priority; 25 to 28 degrees of heel seems about right.

We also have an inclinometer set fore and aft (this should be aligned on the dock before you go racing). As the wind increases most boats tend to sink down by the bows, so move people back to keep her level. But in light winds you don't want the boat too flat because the wetted surface area increases, so move the crew forwards and to leeward to lift the flat stern sections out of the water.

Steering

Wheel steering

The wheel should have plenty of spokes (so you can get hold of it in a seaway) and be covered in something that is comfortable to touch but dries quickly (canvas is ideal). Make sure the gearing suits your style of steering: personally I like an instant response and gear the wheel so that a small movement turns the boat appreciably. Many people like the opposite, however, particularly offwind when it is hard to hold the boat steady. Maxis have two gears, one for upwind and the other for downwind work, but this isn't necessary on a smaller boat.

You should also put a piece of tape around the top of the wheel when the rudder is straight. You (and the trimmers) will find this very useful when judging the angle of weather helm.

Many boats have wheels too small to allow anyone but a contortionist to sit in the right position and still see enough of the boat. In heavy weather you should be able to sit on the weather deck, feet braced and with the wheel between your legs. In medium and light airs you should hang out to leeward in the slot –

45

the wind is accelerated here so you can feel changes better and call for more or less power accordingly. I usually stay to leeward until the wind is strong enough to set the number two, when I move to windward so I can see the waves. The gusts and lulls can now be spotted perfectly well from the windward deck, and I also want my weight to weather.

If the wind and sea stayed constant you would not need to move the wheel at all, and the boat would sail herself perfectly with a steady 5-degree weather helm. But since the wind isn't constant you must move the wheel all the time. Try to feel the wheel as you would a tiller; move it positively but not violently, and remember that the wind only 'sticks' to the sails through a small range of angles of incidence so you *must* respond to each small shift.

As the sea gets up, don't fight the waves – let the boat eat them. She will find her own path through small and medium waves, and you shouldn't be getting any water on deck. If you do, you are luffing into the waves at the wrong moment, so stop pushing her at them. As the waves get higher still, most helmsman luff towards each crest and bear away into the following trough. But beware – if you luff too far and hold the boat too close for too long, the keel stalls and she will slide sideways. If you suspect you are doing this (it is hard to detect) make a conscious effort to bear away earlier on each crest. You can even force yourself to do this by putting more fullness in the genoa and the main – pinching then results in the sails flapping dramatically. If you still have trouble, then check the leading edge of the keel – the shape here is absolutely critical. It usually pays to make it rounder: fine leading edges tend to stall.

'Steering to the compass' to windward is a myth since you should be steering entirely for feel. Have someone check the compass constantly to find the boat's heading, and glance at it occasionally yourself

BEATING IN MEDIUM WINDS

Steering. Wheel steering enables me to sit down to leeward in medium winds (OPPOSITE) rather than steering from the windward deck (RIGHT, TOP). Sitting to leeward with a tiller is fine in light winds (RIGHT) but in anything stronger the helmsman must move to windward (ABOVE).

to see if the wind has headed and you should tack. (The navigator should have written down a bearing for you before he went to sleep, e.g. "more than 245 degrees, tack".)

Tiller steering

A tiller is fine in light and strong winds but you lose out in medium winds because it is difficult to sit down to leeward and push on the tiller extension. You finish up by having to use a foot on the tiller, or giving up and moving back to the windward deck.

Once again, aim for 5 degrees of weather helm to give some lift. If you have more than 5 degrees ease the traveller down, if less move the boom onto the centreline. If you still don't have 5 degrees increase mainsheet tension, and if that isn't enough let off the backstay and tighten the runners to power up the main.

47

Working with the mainsheet trimmer

To windward the person on the mainsheet traveller is essentially steering the boat. The trimmer should watch the helmsman and the tape marker on the wheel: if excessive rudder is needed to keep the boat on course the trimmer moves the traveller down. Once you have worked together for a while there is no need to talk – the trimmer should move the traveller automatically.

Provided it curves down towards the centreline, the traveller needs little pressure to move it, so a simple dinghy system is used. The traveller track should have numbers painted on it every few centimetres so the settings can be repeated on the other tack, and the numbers also help when the traveller is moved back to the medium-wind position after it has been dumped in a gust. Remember: sailing without calibrations is like driving through a strange city without a map – you will never reach your objective.

On 'Yeoman' the trimmer also controls the mainsheet, so the hydraulic pumps are positioned on each side deck where he can work them. Some boats have one winch in the middle, which is not very helpful because the trimmer can't reach it. Fine adjustment to the sheet is carried out using these hydraulics; coarse adjustment is by the usual 4:1 pulley system and jam cleat. There's also a panic button, so the mainsheet can be released quickly in a gust or if the helmsman wants to bear away in a hurry.

A further advantage of the set-up I've described is that the helmsman can work the mainsheet, traveller and wheel by himself, which is very useful for quick, small adjustments offshore.

Using instruments upwind

The helmsman

The helmsman should have a set of dials positioned in his line of sight, and far enough outboard so the trimmer isn't sitting on them. He needs windspeed (apparent), wind direction (apparent), boatspeed and compass.

In daylight, I use boatspeed almost entirely because this tells me how I am taking the waves. I set the delay (which averages out over a time period) according to conditions: if it is rough the instruments update every 15 seconds but in light airs they update every 5 seconds. After a while you will find the boatspeed value 'reads' into your subconscious automatically and you can steer to maximise it.

You should also glance frequently at the windspeed dial to make sure changes in boatspeed have not been caused by an alteration in windstrength. Since it is not possible to keep more than two readings in mind, programme yourself to remember just the boatspeed and windspeed values.

Occasionally you will want to glance at the compass to see if you have been headed or lifted, but mainly I leave this to the crew boss and navigator.

Although the trimmers and the navigator constantly refer to the VMG read-out, the time lag in updating makes it a difficult instrument for the helmsman to use to windward. I tend to get speed up using the boatspeed and wind direction dials, then refer to VMG for confirmation that everything is OK.

So just how do you use the boatspeed read-out to increase speed?

1. Firstly, write down what you're doing now (say 6.25 knots).
2. Then try altering one (and only one) setting.
3. Having made a change, give it time to work. Even though the instruments may only be damped to 5 seconds it takes about a minute for a change to work through, and in most cases the alteration will slow the boat at first. This is because it takes the helmsman time to get used to the new feel of the boat. So don't be too anxious to press on to the next adjustment – you have plenty of time, particularly offshore.
4. If the adjustment increased speed – fine! If not, return to the original setting and try altering another control.

Working with the mainsail trimmer. TOP ROW *Pulling the traveller up helps the boat luff; letting it down (*BOTTOM ROW*) helps her bear away. The aim is for 5° of weather helm (shown by the tape marker on the wheel).*

BEATING IN MEDIUM WINDS

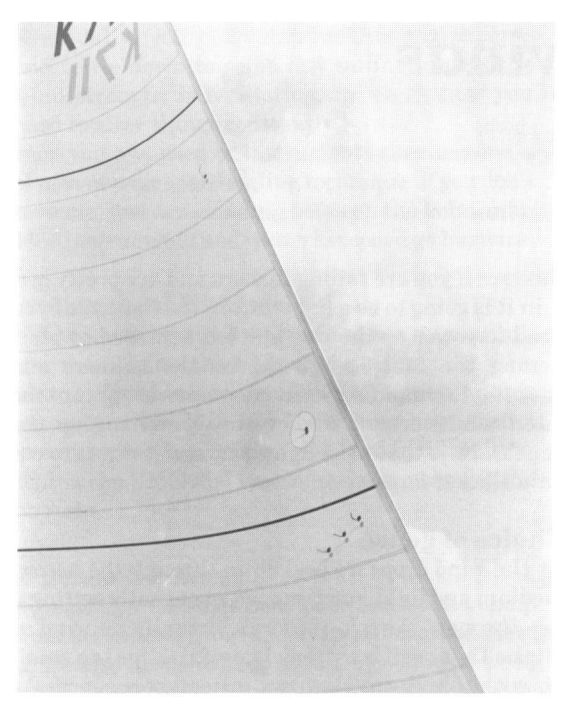

ABOVE *Note the position of the genoa telltales; in light winds use the central pair. A window lets you see the leeward telltale (particularly useful at night) which should be a different colour from the windward one.* OPPOSITE *A full genoa and a narrow slot give the best results in light winds.*

out of the way of the anchor team on the foredeck) and the trimmer holds the Daisy sheet in his hands to feel the wind. This little sail is ideal for accelerating the boat up to about 0.6 knots, when you just have steerage way.

As the wind fills in further we peel to the Norcon but it is always a tense change – if you make it too early the boat slows and you have to peel back and begin again. Too late and you are losing valuable power. Once you are through the 0.6 knot barrier you are away, making (some) of your own wind.

Trimming the genoa
Slacken the genoa halyard and backstay to power up the sail. You want a very full genoa and a narrow slot to keep the wind moving over the back of the main. So ease the genoa sheet a long way (the sail should lie along the lifelines, well away from the shroud) and move the sheet lead right inboard (the sheeting angle can be as small as 5 degrees). Allow the genoa to twist in parallel with the twist in the mainsail.

The sheet lead position is critical. Hold the boat steady and get the trimmer to move the lead inboards slowly while watching the boatspeed. The speed rises rapidly as the lead comes in towards the optimum position, then falls slowly as it is moved too far (and the slot is choked).

Setting the mainsail
Make sure the flattener is fully eased and slacken the outhaul. Pull the traveller well up to weather and ease the sheet to align the boom down the centreline (or, in very light winds, slightly to weather). Do everything possible to increase the curve in the main, and induce twist to keep the leech telltales flying – a light boom is a help here and you may be able to 're-verse' the hydraulic kicker to push up on the boom.

When viewed from the backstay the main should be so full that the leech appears hooked – don't worry, this is quite normal.

In swell
In very light winds when there is still some swell about the sails tend to slat. To counteract this, slacken the genoa sheet a little and lead a tensioned shock cord from the clew to a block on deck. Similarly, rig a strong 'elastic vang' from the boom through a hatch to the heel of the mast (alternatively from the boom to the lee rail). The elastic absorbs some of the shock, allows the sails to set better and lets them 'breathe'.

If the mast is panting tension the runners slightly.

Trim
As the wind drops the crew move first from the weather rail into the middle of the boat, then lie in the slot to leeward, and finally move forward on the lee rail with their boots over the side (ask them to extinguish cigarettes at this point, or the genoa may go

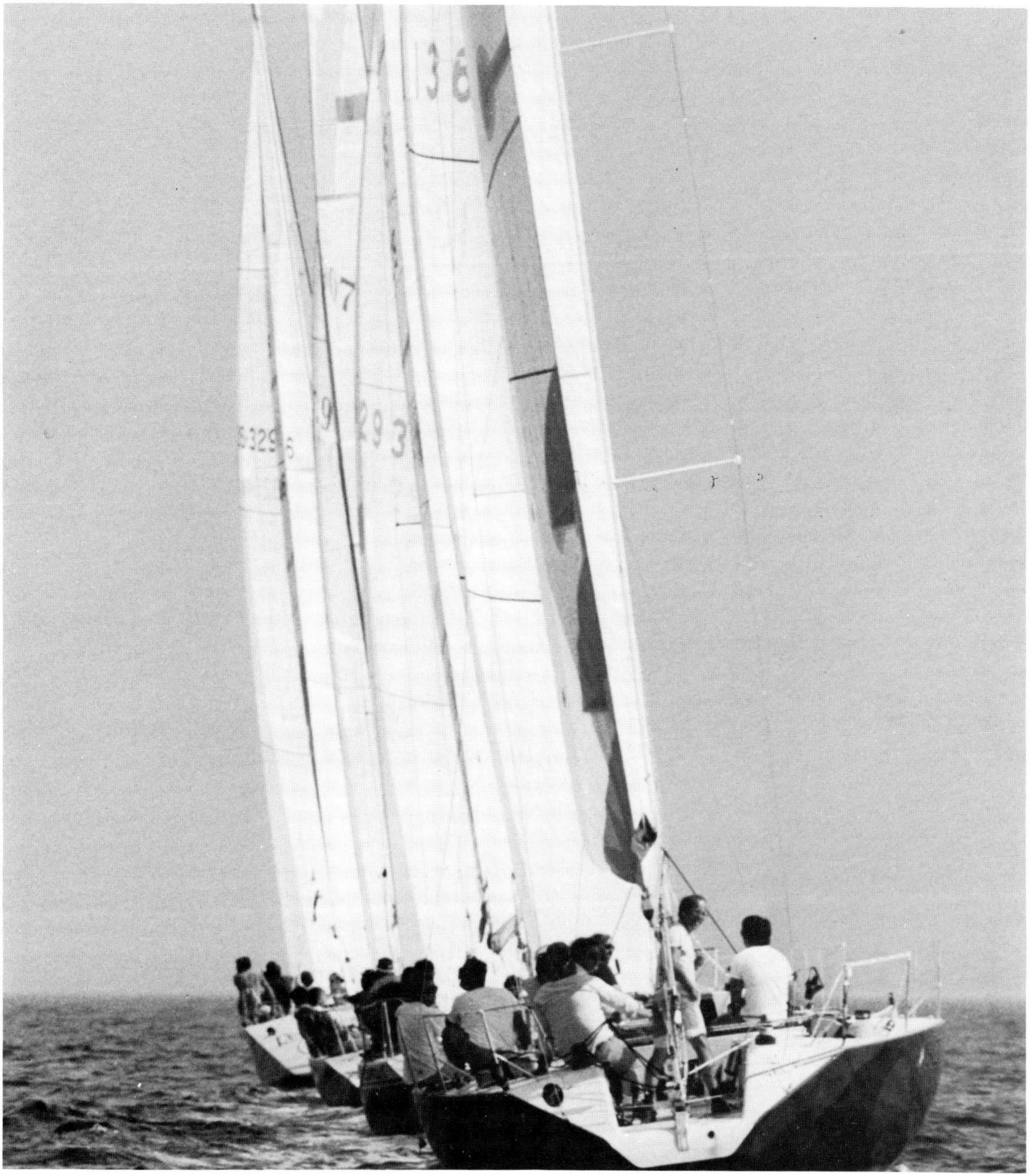

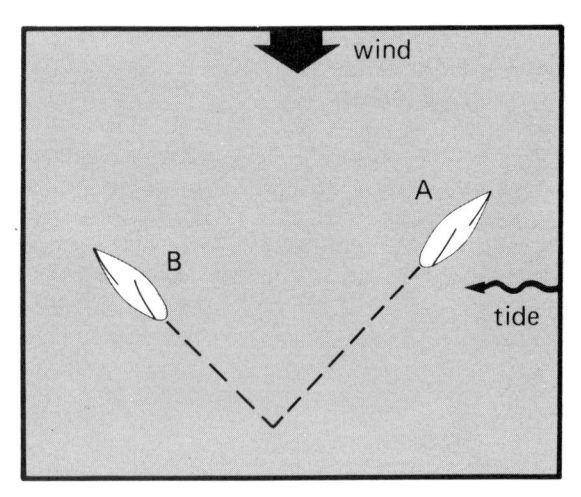

Figure 8.1

up in smoke). Similarly the people down below should be sleeping to leeward and forward.

The ideal is to keep 15 to 20 degrees of leeward heel but you will probably have to settle for 10 degrees in very light airs. Heeling helps the sails hang in the right shape, and moving weight forward lifts the stern out of the water which cuts down skin friction.

Steering

I like to sit to leeward and feel the wind coming through the slot and over my ears (if you don't believe ears are wind-sensitive, pull your hat down lower and watch the boat slow down).

Since there is little feel on the helm to guide you, steer by watching the genoa telltales. Use the pair in the middle of the luff, and watch both the windward and leeward strands (it helps if you have a window in the sail so you can see the leeward one). The aim is to get *both* telltales streaming – the leeward one will break if you are too far off the wind, whilst the windward one goes if you are too close.

Above all, keep the boat moving and don't pinch. If you are prone to this, make the sails even fuller so they will back emphatically when you steer too close to the wind. Offshore, pinching is even more unnecessary because the wind always seems to change before the leg is over and the boats that were sailed high are overtaken on the reach (or run) in to the mark.

If you have a choice, take the tack which has the tide under your lee bow (A not B in figure 8.1). The tide pushes A to the left so her sails are moved through the air and the apparent wind is increased. B is also pushed to the left, but the 'wind' she gains 'blows' onto the leeward side of her sails; her apparent wind is thus reduced.

Tacking on the tide gives an ideal route to windward. Set off like A until the tide turns, then tack so you have the new tide under your lee bow. But whatever else you do, in light winds make sure you arrive uptide of the weather mark – 100 yards (metres) downtide and you could be kedged for hours while the tail-enders round the mark.

Working with the trimmers

The mainsheet and traveller should be fairly static in light winds, and any adjustment is made to trim the leech rather than to aid steering. The genoa sheet trimmer, however, is constantly making alterations, such as winding-in in the gusts to reduce the curve in the sail and allow you to point.

Using instruments

In ghosting conditions wind direction indicators become inaccurate because of the flip-flopping motion of the boat, so rely on the telltales.

Even when there is a breath you will be better off ignoring the instruments – realising that you are only steering, quite rightly, at 45 degrees to the wind is very unsettling and may persuade you to commit the cardinal sin of pinching.

9 · Beating in strong winds

When beating in a blow your main aim is to keep way on so you can work the boat through the waves. You also need to keep the heel to a reasonable level — use the inclinometer and try not to heel more than 25 degrees or you will slide sideways at an alarming rate.

To keep the boat going properly you must have the right sails up for the current windstrength. Pay particular attention to the foresail because it provides the power to pull you through the sea. So if you have a choice of configurations, go for the one that gives the larger foresail and smaller main.

Setting up the rig

Mast bend is not critical when there are reefs in the main; it is far more important to keep the mast in the boat. Ideally the rig should not move at all, so:
1 Use high rig tension.
2 Pull on the runners and then the backstay to bow the middle of the mast forwards a little (the tension that produces this curve prevents the mast whipping and stops it inverting when the boat slams into a wave). But avoid excessive backstay pressure or the mast may crumple.
3 I'm a great believer in safety so I advise keeping both upper runners on (when the reefed main is forward of their line), in case one breaks. Tension the vang so that if the mainsheet goes the boom won't fly up in the air; also, if someone falls over the side it is hard to spin round onto the reach if the vang is off.

Sadly masts do sometimes break, but as helmsman you can help prevent extra damage. If you think the mast is going to break luff to take the strain off it, but if it is actually falling down bear away so it lands in the water, not on deck (and, most important, not on the crew).

Reefing pennants

We always sail with the first reefing pennant rigged, but the lines for the second and third are only reeved when needed. This is made easier by rigging a complete loop of light nylon line (nylon is strong, but does stretch a bit) between the first and second cringle on

RIGHT *We use a nylon 'mouse' to pull the reefing pennant through its cringles.*

BEATING IN STRONG WINDS

the leech, and another loop between the second and third cringle. With the first reef in it is a simple matter to use the nylon mouse to pull the number two pennant through its cringle and make fast. The process is repeated when going from the second to the third reef.

Jib sheets
Use J-clips to attach the sheets to the genoa: it is dangerous to use knots because they can jam on the rigging during a tack and take the mast out of the boat. Also, marking your sheets to help gauge trim will only work if the point of attachment doesn't vary. Make sure the clips won't fly open when the jib flogs.

Clothing
Try to avoid having everyone below putting on oilskins as the first squall hits you. If the wind is obviously getting up have waterproofs passed up so everyone can get dressed on deck. Above 20 knots everyone will need oilskins and above 30 knots they should also be wearing harnesses and lifejackets.

Through the gears
Now let's suppose the wind is gradually increasing from 15 knots to hurricane level, forcing us to reduce power in the rig. The notes that follow show the way we reduce sail on 'Yeoman', though you will have to work out the best programme for your own boat since each one is different.

Wind 15 to 19 knots apparent: full main and heavy number one. Flattener progressively pulled on. Runners eased off, babystay pulled on and backstay tensioned to bend mast. Traveller gradually eased down to prevent excessive heel, and genoa sheet lead moved to leeward to keep slot open (if necessary, the sheet lead can be moved aft as well to open the slot still further). Genoa leech line slackened to prevent 'hooking'.

As the wind increases you will find:
- The lee rail is in the water.
- You can see the boat slipping sideways.
- Boatspeed and VMG are dropping.
- The main is very flat, and beginning to backwind so badly that it vibrates.
- The windspeed exceeds the cut-off figure you determined in practice for full sail.

Now is the time for the first peel.

Wind 19 to 21 knots: full main and number two. Peel to the number two genoa, with the sheet lead on the inboard track. Whenever you set a smaller genoa always sheet it close to the centreline at first, then gradually barber-haul it outboard as the wind increases. Adjust the mainsheet traveller to keep 5 degrees of weather helm and the boat driving through the waves.

Wind 21 to 25 knots: first reef and number two. Take in the first reef to reduce heel and keep the boat balanced.

25 to 30 knots: first reef and number three. By this time the seas are getting large. Peel to the number three — waves breaking into a large genoa will either rip it or carry away the whole rig. As before, gradually barber-haul the foresail from its initial inboard position.

Wind 30 to 35 knots: second reef and number three. Eventually you will find you have to feather the boat to keep her upright, but her speed drops so the seas stop her. Now is the time to put in the second reef. Everyone should now be wearing harnesses and be clipped on. Despite the fact that a good helmsman never lets waves flop on board, close the hatches.

Wind 35 to 40 knots: second reef and number four. Peel to number four.

Wind 40 to 50 knots: third reef and number four. Put in the third reef. As soon as the leech of the main is clear of the runners, pull on all the runners in case one breaks or in case a wave suddenly knocks you round onto the other tack. Similarly each jib must, from now on, have four jibsheets because they tend to break in strong winds.

BEATING IN STRONG WINDS

ABOVE The flattener depowers the main to windward. Note the 'toast-rack' arrangement for positioning the genoa leads.

Wind 50 knots plus: third reef and storm jib. When setting the storm jib tie a piece of line through each luff eye and around the headfoil. It is an absolute must to lash the head cringle around the headfoil, because the aft pull on the head is huge. Alternatively use a D-shaped shackle to attach the head to the headfoil. Finally, lash the tack cringle to the forestay. All this should prevent the jib pulling off the forestay — in a storm it is very difficult to get it back on board.

More extreme conditions: trisail and storm jib/ storm jib alone. Take down the main, lash it to the boom and lash the boom to the deck. Then set the trisail loose-footed, sheeting it with the leeward spinnaker sheet. Some people advocate sheeting the trisail to the boom, but in my experience this is difficult to rig up — and that boom is very solid when it is flying about.

In the 1979 Fastnet we were finally forced to drop even the trisail, and 'beat' under storm jib alone. It is perfectly possible (though uncomfortable) to make ground to windward in this way.

The frequency of sail changing depends entirely on the weather — you simply have to change as often as is required, even if that means activity every quarter-hour.

If the wind is up and down, leave the old sail in a

bundle along the *weather* deck so it can be used again. Even if the wind is rising (or falling) rapidly, go through each 'gear change' rather than skipping a step — your foredeck work should be slick enough to cope, and there is nothing worse than sitting with small sails up waiting for a wind increase.

Types of peel

On our boat the foredeck decides on the type of peel we are going to do. There is no doubt that a tack change* is quickest, so before you call a peel think carefully about whether you can afford to tack, and tell the foredeck your decision. Sometimes it is even worth doing a double tack change, i.e tack-hoist-tack-drop, with the foredeck calling the time.

If you can't tack and are forced to do a side-by-side change the most helpful thing the helmsman can do is to keep steering a straight course, although bearing away slightly (and easing the genoa sheet) may help unstick the two headsails as one is pulled down. It may also help to unfasten the tack of the old sail, holding it in place by the spinnaker downhaul attached to the cunningham eye. This opens a large gap which allows the new sail to be hoisted more easily.

Trim

Most modern boats have their widest point well back, with little buoyancy in the bows. So as the wind increases move everyone aft to increase stability, stop the bows burying and increase waterline length.

Steering through waves

Look carefully at the direction the waves are moving: often this is quite different from the wind direction, particularly if the wind has shifted recently. If this is the case choose the tack that takes you along the waves, rather than the one that slams you head-on into them. The waves will gradually take on the new wind direction, so when you tack later you will find you have an easier time — in other words this tactic gives a gain on *both* tacks.

Luff slightly as the boat climbs each wave and begin to bear off at the moment the bow cuts the crest, steering down into the trough. Choosing the right moment to bear away is the secret, and once you have got it right the motion improves — the correct course gives the least pounding and the least water on board. (In fact it is easy to tell from down below how the helmsman is doing.) Note that you should be steering in this way over every wave, so you need to concentrate hard and move the helm constantly.

Big waves have smaller waves on top, the little ones being irregular. Try to guide the boat along the face of the large wave, luff through the crest at the lowest point and then bear away quickly into the

---

* See *Yacht Crewing* by Malcolm McKeag in this series.

trough beyond. Above all, don't let the large seas push the bow off to leeward or the boat will heel as she climbs the crest and you won't dare to bear away at the top. The hull then drops straight into the trough and stops.

Note that there is no chance of steering a compass course because your main concern is getting through the waves, so ask someone else to watch the heading. Beware also of steering for too long in strong winds unless your other helmsman isn't good in these conditions: two to three hours is plenty.

Working with the mainsheet trimmer
Easing down the traveller (and barber-hauling the genoa) should reduce weather helm to a sensible level — it is impossible to steer through waves if you are fighting the helm. However in very strong winds you may need to pull the traveller inboard a little to give more feel because there is so little sail up.

In less than 25 knots of wind the trimmer should help you work each wave by letting the traveller down as you luff towards the crest, pulling it back up as you bear away towards the trough.

Above 25 knots this isn't feasible, but between 35 and 45 knots you may occasionally need help as you pick your way over the lowest part of the crests. Above 45 knots the traveller just stays in the same place because the pressure on it is so great.

The mainsheet needs to be tight. In very strong winds, however, you may need to induce twist in the main to keep the boat going and prevent her stalling, so tension the vang and let off the mainsheet a little.

In stronger winds the crews' weight should be aft to stop the bows burying and to increase waterline length.

10 · Tacking

Tacking is the manoeuvre you will carry out most often, so it is the one where practice pays the greatest dividend. Obviously you want to keep your speed up as much as possible, but in practice you will always lose at least a couple of lengths every time you go about. Careful preparation helps reduce this loss to a minimum.

When to tack

One of the most important skills to windward is keeping in phase with the windshifts. We have already seen that the navigator is constantly plotting true wind direction against time, and he can use this plot to keep you synchronised with the shifts. If the wind was oscillating as shown in figure 10.1 you would tack at the times marked. You can also use the plot to help with tactics — if you were on port tack at X and approaching a boat on starboard it would pay to tack rather than duck her stern — because you are going to want to tack in a moment anyway. But if you had to make the decision at Y, ducking would be the answer, because port tack will be favoured for some time.

If you get out of phase with the shifts or are confused about what the wind is doing, stay on one tack until the sequence is sorted out.

Preparation

Let's suppose the tactician has called for a tack.
1. Firstly check that you have room to go about — i.e. there are no boats or obstructions close to weather.
2. Next think about the crew: do you have enough people on deck to tack properly? Do you want the halyards wound up (it is much easier to do this during a tack when the strain comes off the rig)? Should someone pump the bilges (much more effective when the boat is level)? If in doubt, get another couple of crew members on deck, but note that tacking is the only major manoeuvre where some people can stay below.
3. The crew off watch will have to change sides anyway! Have the crew boss warn them so they can move across just before the boat tacks. On our boat each bunk pivots and its angle to the horizontal is controlled by a block and tackle; it is much easier to wind yourself up with the boat on the old tack. (Actually you won't have any trouble persuading

Figure 10.1

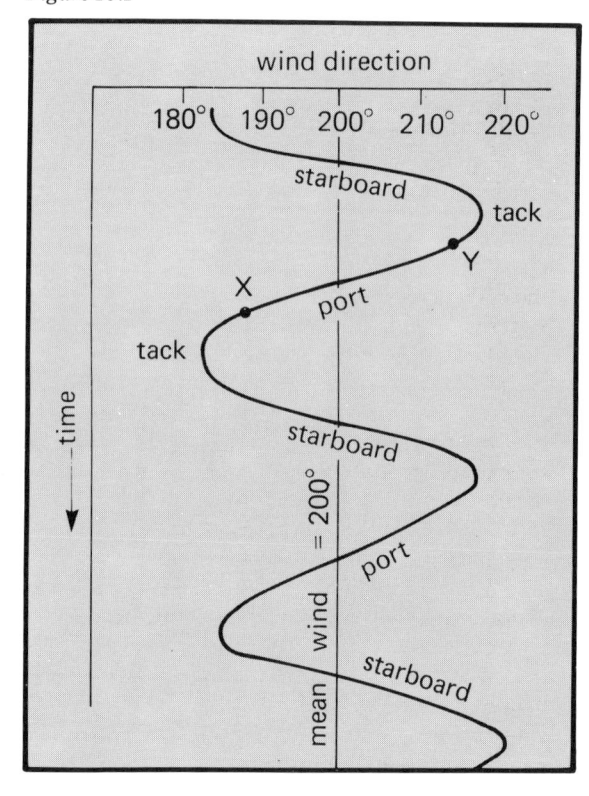

Preparing to tack.

the crew to move across smartly because the bilge water pours into the leeward bunks.)
4 Check that the new genoa sheet lead is in the same position as you are using on the current tack.
5 Note the positions of the traveller and runners so they can be set in the same way on the new tack.
6 In medium or light winds let the babystay go so the genoa doesn't catch on it as you tack. But if the wind is too strong (i.e. you can't let off the babystay because you're afraid of the mast inverting) attach the spinnaker downhaul to the eye halfway along the foot of the genoa and detail someone to pull on it at the right moment. This concertinas the sail forward during the tack and stops it damaging itself on the babystay.
7 Have a good look at your boatspeed and remember it as a target for the new tack.
8 Stand up and look ahead to find a smooth bit of water to tack in. Try to tack in the *bottom* of the smallest trough you can find.
9 Check the compass at the last moment to make sure you haven't been lifted.
10 Call "ready about" and prepare to turn.

Helming through a tack

Always try to tack the same way and at the same speed so everyone gets used to the pace. If you sling the boat round too fast then at best it will be hard to get the genoa in properly. At worst it will be caught aback and she will swing too far, heel over and stop. But it is equally bad to tack too slowly because the genoa flogs itself to death on the mast and shrouds. So find the optimum turning speed and stick to it. To tack:

TACKING

Activity in the cockpit during a tack.

1. Bear off slightly (no need to ease the sheets) to make sure you have enough speed. Beginning off the wind also lengthens the tack, which gives everyone more time to work in.
2. By now you will have a lot of weather helm; simply straighten up and the boat will swing up into the wind.
3. Start to steer her round by turning the wheel 10 to 20 degrees. The genoa sheet should not be let go until the sail is pushed back onto the shroud: this instant of backwinding will also help push the bow round.
4. If you are inshore begin to centralise the wheel when the boat is head to wind. But offshore hold the wheel over until you are sure the boat has tacked, because it is hopeless if you get stuck in irons and downright dangerous if you let a wave knock you back onto the old tack (ripping the genoa and breaking the battens in the main).

When you are judging the moment to straighten up, aim to turn a little 'too far' — say about 5 degrees past the close-hauled course.

5. Trim the sails to this 'free' heading, then watch the boatspeed dial carefully. For some reason the speed seems to go up as you begin to turn, then drops during the tack. As soon as it begins to go up again start to luff slowly to close-hauled, giving the trimmers time to wind in the sheets.
6. Your speed should now be the same as on the old tack. If not, check your steering, then the rig.

How often to tack?

Inshore you often find yourself short-tacking along the bank to dodge a foul tide. Your problem is knowing how far out to go on each leg. The answer depends on the time your boat takes to regain speed after a tack. Find this out during a practice session — in

'Yeoman' it is about 90 seconds. Having tacked and got up to speed you need to sail for at least as long again before going about. For us this means tacking not more than once every three minutes.

If you are short-tacking with another boat the temptation is to go about every time she approaches so you stay inside her. But if this means tacking more frequently than the optimum, duck her transom and keep sailing fast. When you meet next you should be ahead, and can then sail your own race.

Tacking in light winds

Light-wind genoas are delicate so you should definitely let off the babystay and detail someone to walk forwards with the clew of the sail at the beginning of the tack, letting it go only when it will blow clear of the new leeward shroud. It can then be wound in gently by the trimmer.

The crew can roll tack as they would a dinghy: begin with everyone to leeward and ask them to move across as you begin to turn. This should fan the sails through the air and help keep speed up.

There is no need to bear away before you begin: simply luff very gently into the tack, almost shooting head to wind. Then turn slowly onto a close reach, wait for as long as is needed to pick up speed, and finally luff back to close-hauled.

Tacking in strong winds

Tack in the same way as for medium winds, but never let off the babystay. You will probably be using a small jib and it won't be damaged, particularly if the trimmer releases the sheet late in the tack so the jib 'wipes' across the babystay.

As helmsman don't forget to unclip your safety harness before you tack, and hook back on when you're safely on the new course. Otherwise you will be trapped to leeward, much to the opposition's amusement.

It is vital to get the crew across onto the windward deck (with their boots out) as quickly as possible to give the boat some power, but remember that tacking is a dangerous time and people can become disorientated and go over the side. So make sure they clip on immediately they arrive on the new deck.

11 · The weather mark

For a perfect rounding of the windward mark you tack bang on the layline, judge the rounding perfectly and have the spinnaker drawing immediately. Needless to say it doesn't always go like that!

The navigator's job
Rouse the navigator as soon as the mark is sighted.

His first job is to make sure it is the right buoy (so that even if a neighbouring boat suddenly reaches off to another mark, you have the confidence to stand on towards your original choice).

Next he needs to calculate the tidal flow, so you can judge accurately when to tack for the mark. Alternatively, the computer can input the tidal effect and automatically calculate the ideal course. Lastly he should calculate what the wind's speed and direction will be on the next leg so the right sails can be prepared.

Planning your approach
Unless the mark is close inshore, approach it as though you are beating inside a 10-degree cone (figure 11.1); note that your tacks become more frequent as the buoy comes nearer. If one side is favoured (figure 11.2) beat up that side of the cone.

Ten or fifteen minutes before the mark everyone should be up on deck and getting acclimatised — it is impossible for the crew to do a major job if they are bleary-eyed.

Having calculated the wind on the next leg, the

Figure 11.1

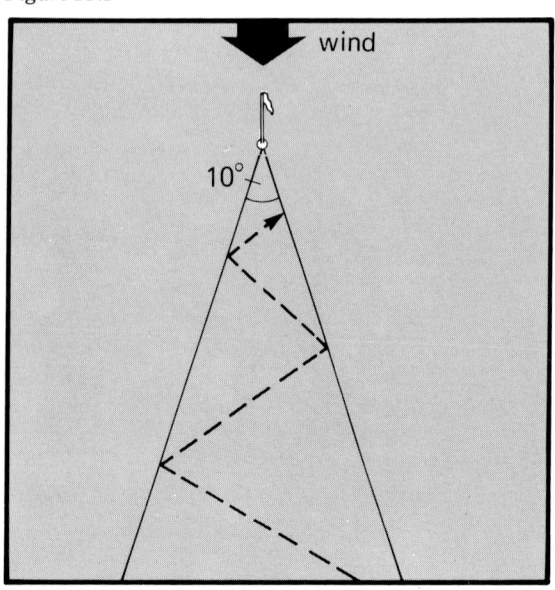

Figure 11.2

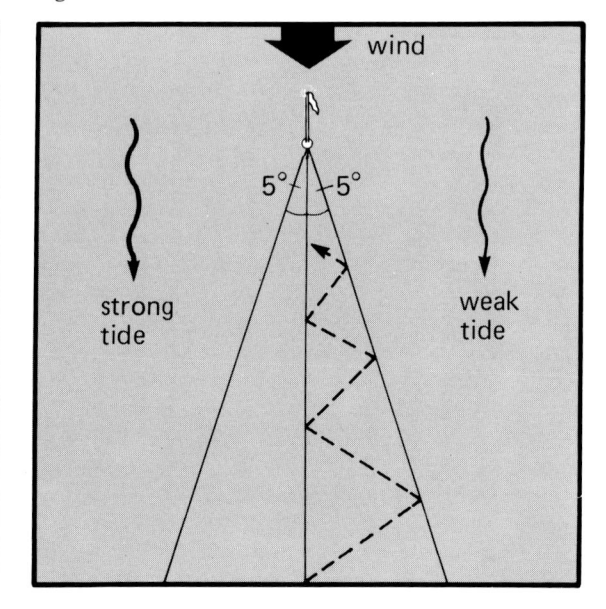

navigator can assess from his chart the sails needed. The crew boss then details someone to bring them on deck.

Try to stay away from the layline until you are about 200 yards (metres) from the mark. When you do tack be sure to overstand a little because the last thing you want is a double tack near the buoy. This prevents your putting up the spinnaker pole in advance, and is sure to lead to a slow, confused rounding.

For the same reasons, avoid a tack set — for example approaching on port, tacking onto starboard and bearing away immediately round the mark.

Position the spinnaker sheet leads (forward or aft, as required) before the mark. Tie the leeward runner forward out of the way. If the reach will be tight organise the jockey pole.

The choice of spinnaker halyard is determined by the peels that may be needed on the next leg.

Don't set the spinnaker pole until you are sure you can lay the mark without tacking. Check this either by taking a transit on the shore, or if there is no land in sight, by taking a bearing on the buoy.

The rounding

The spinnaker is hoisted as the boat arrives at the mark, the order being given by the helmsman (since he is the only person who can see the buoy properly). The danger of hoisting too early is wrapping the kite round the mark.

Our spinnaker always goes up stopped with elastic bands. This is much easier (and therefore quicker) than trying to hoist a kite half-full of wind. The only exceptions are the light spinnakers.

The hydraulics (vang and backstay) and runners are also adjusted *on* rounding. Remember that if the vang is left on tight the boom may break.

If the reach is tight move any spare crew aft and onto the weather rail, to be joined by everyone else as soon as the sails are sorted out. If you still feel the boat is overpowered bear away (before the broaching starts) and make your adjustments — such as moving the spinnaker sheet lead aft, moving the pole back and letting the vang off a little.

If you're doing a gybe set — i.e. bearing away to a

When rounding in close company decide if you want to luff after the mark. If so, delay setting the kite. If not, as here, go for a fast hoist.

THE WEATHER MARK

run, gybing, *then* putting up the kite — don't turn too fast. Pause before gybing to make sure everyone is ready; a broach now could slew the boat round onto the mark. (Having slogged all that way to windward, this is not a popular time to get disqualified!)

On a tight rounding beware of 'arcing'. If you are racing around navigation marks they can be 30 or 40 feet (9 to 12 metres) high, and if the buoy and your mast roll in opposite directions they can collide from a range of 60 feet (18 metres). I've even seen a boat with her mast trapped through the railings of the Royal Sovereign light vessel — difficult to untangle, that one!

Just once in a while, though, you have to take a chance at the weather mark. In the 1975 Admiral's Cup we were racing in very light winds. The whole fleet was just stemming the tide and trying to round Prince Consort buoy. It was clear that whoever rounded first would be able to scoot off inshore and win the race, but although we got tantalisingly close to the mark several times we were swept back on each occasion. Finally I plucked up courage and steered 'Yeoman' straight around the buoy: as we drifted broadside onto it a cushion of water built up between the hull and the mark and pushed our stern off and around. We'd done it! As dark fell we crossed the Squadron line, and hundreds of people cheered as the winning gun boomed out. An unforgettable moment, but an extra barnacle on that windward mark would have turned victory into disaster.

TOP ROW *A tack set makes life difficult for the crew because the pole cannot be raised in advance.* BOTTOM ROW *Here the pole is ready; as the boat rounds the kite is hoisted and broken out in seconds.*

12 · Reaching

Unless you are racing on an Olympic triangle a good proportion of your sailing time will be spent on the reach; indeed, on some offshore races you can reach all the way round the course. So good reaching speed is a vital race-winning factor.

In the first part of this chapter I look at the technique for medium winds; later on I describe the differences for light and strong winds.

Setting up the rig
The mast should be raked forwards, but with a slight aft bend. This can be achieved by letting off some of the backstay tension (never free it right off) and then adjusting the vang until the helmsman is happy with the feel of the boat.

Should we set the spinnaker (and staysail)?
In deciding whether or not the kite will pay, the angle and strength of the wind are everything. If you have a reaching spinnaker, think about setting it if the apparent wind is 60 degrees off the bow or more. Don't let the course to the next mark affect your decision too much: if the navigator calculates that by bearing off 5 degrees you can set the kite and still get to the mark quicker, go for it. And if in doubt offshore, do bear away: you'll almost certainly gain because the wind will probably change before you get to the mark. The alternative is to luff early, then set the spinnaker and reach down to the buoy; because of the chance of the wind changing later I hardly ever do this, unless there is a tide advantage on the high course.

If you decide that it is a spinnaker leg, bear away to help the crew hoist. Stay on a broad reach until the boat has picked up speed and the gear is fully sorted out, then luff slowly back on course (or as high on the wind as you judge to be safe).

Offshore it seldoms pays to screw the boat up into the wind with the kite pulled in tight and the main flapping, because the boat simply slips sideways. If you think you have this problem look back at the wake: if you can see it disappearing upwind you are probably better off without the spinnaker.

If the boat needs more power, set a staysail. But if the boat is on the verge of broaching leave the staysail in its bag (guaranteed to please the foredeck!) because it will only heel the boat over and make her luff.

Steering on a spinnaker reach
Stand on the windward side of the wheel (or sit to weather if you are using a tiller). Make sure the crew moved smartly up to weather and aft as the kite filled, then work to reduce weather helm to a reasonable level.

Firstly, the mainsheet trimmer can help by letting out more sheet as the boat starts to luff up. (He will normally have the traveller right down, and be trimming to the telltales on the luff of the main.)

In a similar way the trimmer on the spinnaker sheet can ease when he feels the boat beginning to heel.

Lastly, the controls can be adjusted to depower the rig if weather helm is still excessive.

If the waves are small simply steer to the spinnaker. Although the trimmers are constantly adjusting the sheet and guy you can help by steering to keep the luff just lifting. If a major shift arrives alter course to keep the spinnaker full while the guy is reset.

If the kite does collapse make sure the staysail is dumped immediately, because the spinnaker won't fill again in its lee.

A shy spinnaker reach.

If the waves are large enough for surfing (or surging), work hard to ride them.

1. Luff a little to gain speed as the wave approaches.
2. As the transom is lifted sheet in hard.
3. Sheet out and bear away to surf down the wave's face.
4. As the boat picks up speed sheet in (the apparent wind will come forward).
5. Smaller boats can pump their sheets to promote surfing, but excessive pumping is illegal.

Sometimes the waves are running at the wrong angle for surfing. Consider luffing above the rhumb line (or bearing away below it) to give yourself a better chance of catching a ride. Offshore the deviation will often be worth while, as the wind may change during the leg anyway.

Another nice way of getting about the ocean is catching a tow on a faster boat's wake. Indeed small boats often begin lining up on the stern of a bigger boat well before the start. With luck they will be towed for miles before being shaken off.

To catch a ride during the race wait for a slightly faster boat to overtake (don't choose someone who is *too* fast). Encourage her to come by to windward and luff so you end up on her leeward quarter (avoid riding on her weather quarter-wave because this threatens her wind and she will take action sooner to get rid of you). The best effect is on the first wave behind her transom, but the second wave would do. Once in position simply steer to keep your bow pointing downhill — and enjoy the ride.

If you are in the faster boat there are several ways to avoid hitchhikers.

69

- As the other boat luffs onto your wake, luff too; this keeps enough distance between you to stop her catching your wake.
- If this fails try bearing away onto a run: your quarter-wave is now much reduced and the opposition will soon drop back.
- Finally, watch for a buoy and steer straight for it so your spinnaker hides it from the tow. Steer round it at the last moment, forcing her to swerve violently and lose speed. By the time she has sorted herself out, you are long gone.

Final checks

Use the boatspeed read-out to check your performance. If we are going slowly I generally look at:
1. Our trim. No one should be sleeping to leeward and the navigator should be up on deck, preferably aft on the weather rail with the rest of the crew.
2. The spinnaker clews. They should be the same height; if not, the pole is too high (or too low).
3. The lead for the spinnaker sheet. Move it forwards or aft until speed increases.
4. The mainsail. If it is too flat the boat will be underpowered. But if it is too full the mainsheet will have to be trimmed excessively.

Using the staysail with the spinnaker

On a broad reach we generally have the staysail set. In fact once the blooper comes down the staysail goes up, the objective being simply to catch more wind. Fix the tack as far to windward as possible so the luff is just off the spinnaker pole (as the pole moves forward the tack can come in towards the centreline). Then trim the staysail sheet in the same way as for a normal foresail.

White-sail reaching

By this I mean sailing off the wind, but not far enough off for a spinnaker. Barber-haul the genoa to the rail and forward, which tightens the leech and forms a slot. Make the main as full as possible by letting off the outhaul and backstay, and by adjusting the vang carefully. The trimmer then lets the mainsheet out

ABOVE *Setting a staysail can give more power on the reach.*

RIGHT *In light winds the spinnaker trimmer moves to leeward so we can talk. In very light airs I often take the spinnaker sheet myself.*

slowly, watching the boatspeed read-out and adjusting for maximum speed. Note that this will *not* be with the front of the main just flapping (as the older textbooks used to describe) — this is much too far out for speed.

Finally, check the helm: if you have too much weather helm flatten the main or let out the mainsheet.

Double-headed rig

Double-headed reaching is much more difficult than people think because you have to make two slots work. I can only suggest you adjust the foresails and main watching the boatspeed carefully; once the boat is in the groove leave the sheets and steer to the telltales on the genoa.

Light wind reaching

Sit to leeward and watch the luff of the spinnaker. The sheet and guy should be kept fairly still while you steer to keep the spinnaker full. In very light winds it helps if the spinnaker trimmer moves to leeward so you can talk. But in a real drifter I like to take the sheet myself and steer to it.

When white-sail reaching in light winds the staysail won't work, so set up the main and genoa for speed and then steer to the telltales on the genny.

Strong wind reaching

As the wind increases you need to reduce power in the rig. Let's suppose that we are reaching under staysail, 0.75 oz spinnaker and main and the wind is steadily coming up. The list below shows how we move 'through the gears' on 'Yeoman', each change being made when the helmsman feels that a broach is likely.
1 Lower the staysail.
2 Peel to the 1.5 oz spinnaker, and rehoist the staysail.
3 Begin dumping the main by easing the mainsheet.
4 Dump the main by using the vang.
5 Lower the staysail. Repeat steps 3 and 4.

REACHING

Broaching is not inevitable! See the advice on this page.

6 If you can bear off, do so. If not, peel to the 2.2 oz bullet-proof (i.e. the 80 per cent spinnaker).
7 Set the number two genoa and staysail and lower the spinnaker. Attach the spinnaker topping lift to the middle of the genoa foot to raise the bottom of the sail clear of the waves.
8 Lower the staysail.
9 Peel to the number three genoa (and full main, flattened right off).
10 Put in the first, then the second, reef in the main.
11 Peel to the number four genoa. Two reefs in the main.

Broaching

Modern boats are wide in the middle and sharp at the front. When they heel the bow drops and behaves like a wedge pushing through the water, forcing the bow up into the wind. As this happens the flow of water over the rudder is broken, and cavitation results. By this time the boat is over on her ear, and to add to the helmsman's problems the rudder is lifted clear of the water. He is helpless to prevent the broach continuing.

Although it looks spectacular in yachting calendars, broaching is not recommended. Here are a few ideas which may help you avoid it.

1 Here someone briefed to watch over the quarter for gusts (i.e. for dark patches moving over the sea). He calls "gust coming" in good time.
2 As the boat begins to heel the spinnaker trimmer bangs out about 3 feet (a metre) of sheet. (Note that he doesn't ease it gently, but dumps it *fast*.) The boat comes upright immediately and the bow lifts.

3 Bear away quickly.
4 If this doesn't work let the mainsheet off.
5 If you still have problems release the vang.
6 If necessary, dump the staysail.
7 If she is still out of control dump the spinnaker completely, straighten the helm briefly (to stop rudder cavitation) then bear away.

Recovering from a bad broach
Despite all this you are bound to broach sometimes. With the boat on her side you may wonder if she is ever going to come up again! What you do next depends on the rig and the size of the boat.

On a large yacht:
1 Pull in the staysail to pull her head off the wind.
2 Sheet in the main to regain speed and traction.
3 Finally sheet home the spinnaker.

On a yacht without a staysail you may have to hoist a jib or take down the spinnaker before she will bear away.

On a small boat pull in the spinnaker briefly (with the main still flapping) to get her head off, then quickly let it out again.

White-sail reaching in strong winds
The main objective (other than speed) is to keep the boat upright. Set the number two genoa (the number one would rip in the waves), barber-haul it outboard and cleat the sheet. Set the main like a blade by cranking down on the vang, then play the mainsheet to prevent excessive heel and weather helm.

Some common faults
- Don't let the crew overtrim the sails. It is less work like this (because the sails are always full of wind, and look pretty) but speed on the reach comes from constant adjustment to sheeting angles.
- Don't steer straight. Luff up in the lulls and bear away in the puffs. Move with the wind.
- Watch carefully for gusts and react quickly to avoid broaching.

13 · Gybing

Most people approach gybing with a certain amount of caution, and it has to be said that this is probably the most dangerous manoeuvre. Yet the crew who can gybe smartly are not only safe, but will gain valuable ground over their sloppier rivals. In this chapter I suggest how the skipper and the helmsman can make the whole process easier for the crew. Since the dip-pole gybe is probably the most common, that is the one described here, although much of what I say applies to other gybing methods.

Preparation
Try to allow plenty of preparation time: five minutes is none too long. As with any major manoeuvre, everyone should be on deck and the whole crew briefed so they know exactly what to do.

Mainsheet. Decide whether the trimmer is going to wind in the mainsheet slowly (and let it out gently), or whether he is going to let it bang across. On 'Yeoman' we tend to wind in slowly (to give the runner man time to work), but there is a danger of the boat being slewed round by a wave when the main is on the centreline, which is bound to cause a broach.

Banging the boom over is fine if it works, but often the main comes halfway and then swings back to the old side again, which confuses the runner man — not to mention the helmsman.

Mast. The best way to break a mast while gybing is to allow the middle to bow backwards. You can prevent this in two ways.
- Firstly put on sufficient backstay tension to bend the middle of the mast forwards.
- Secondly, rig a gybing strop. This is a wire which takes the place of the babystay (which has to be taken off before you gybe). The strop runs from the mast end of the spinnaker pole to the middle of the foredeck, and becomes tight when the pole is raised to its normal height on the mast. The strop pulls forwards on the mast and stops it inverting.

Sheets and guys. Check that the lazy guy has been taken forward so it can be clipped on to the pole as it swings under the forestay. Make sure too that the lazy sheet is rigged over the top of the spinnaker pole, or the pole can't be tripped.

Controlling the pole. Remind the man on the topping lift that he is to lower the rope to its mark as the pole is gybed. (If he drops the pole too far it will hit the deck, but if it isn't lowered enough it will hit the forestay and probably kink it: then the genoa can't be hoisted.)

Similarly, point out the mark on the mast which shows how far to raise the pole before the gybe begins.

Runners. Make sure the new runner is underneath the boom — if it is over the top the boom will catch as it comes across.

If everything is OK take a deep breath, stand where you can duck low enough, and call the gybe.

The gybe

From the helmsman's point of view the secret of a good gybe is simply to take it easy. Don't make a tight turn unless you are sandwiched by other boats: a gentle sweep greatly reduces the chance of a broach.

The faster you are sailing on a run, the less the force on the sails. It follows that the best time to gybe is when you are surfing flat out down a wave, even

ABOVE *The moment of truth: suddenly all that gybing practice seems worth while.* BELOW *A good foredeck hand can snap the new guy in place as the pole swings past the bow in a continuous arc.*

75

A dip-pole gybe in light weather. (1) The lazy guy is clipped on (it is removed in light airs). (2) The bowman takes the lazy guy to the bow while the sheet trimmer pulls in hard on the new sheet. (3) The pole is tripped by the mast hand. (4) The topping lift is dropped to its set

though this may seem to be the most dramatic moment. So begin your turn as a good wave picks you up. Then:
1. Turn *gently*.
2. As the boom is wound in make sure the new runner is pulled on (but not too tight).
3. Call "trip" *before* the boat heads straight downwind, but not until you are sure she is going to gybe. The pole is swung forward, the new guy clipped on and the pole raised again on the new side.
4. The foredeck crew reattaches the babystay (undoing the gybing strop can wait till later).
5. You should now be surfing straight downwind with the boom on the centreline. The old runner is eased out as the boom runs out to the new side (if this runner isn't let off it catches the boom and may cause a broach).
6. A yacht will often try to turn back downwind at this point, so steer firmly on through the gybe. There is no need to reverse the helm at this point (as you would on a dinghy).
7. Straighten up on a very broad reach (don't turn any further for the moment).
8. The spinnaker pole is pulled down at the mast end to its new reaching position.
9. Everyone runs back to the weather quarter (it is very dicey to luff with weight forward).
10. The spinnaker sheet and guy must have pressure on them before you continue your turn. Have someone let off the vang a bit if a broach looks possible, then luff slowly onto the new reaching course.
11. Breathe out — you made it!

Making a crash gybe

If you are boxed in and have to do a tight gybe, the priorities are:
1. To turn as slowly as possible.
2. To get the new runner on.
3. To get the boom across and *right out* to the new side so that if the boat broaches she has little pressure at the stern.
4. To make sure the spinnaker trimmer is ready on the new sheet (and the new lazy guy is free) so he can let the kite flag if the boat starts to broach.

4   5   6

mark. This allows the pole to swing to the bow where the bowman clips on the new guy. (5) The bowman pushes the pole outboard as the topping lift and new guy are pulled in (6) With the spinnaker setting nicely on the new side the bowman moves aft.

Sorting out problems

All sorts of things can go wrong during a gybe, but the main problems seem to be:

- The foredeck man fails to clip the guy onto the pole as it sweeps across. If this happens carry on with the gybe but stay on a run once the main has gone across and get the pole back down on deck fast. Then rig the guy and hoist the pole again.
- The sail doesn't trip. In this case keep going on the old gybe until it *is* tripped.
- The main doesn't come across, or for some reason the main and spinnaker pole end up on the same side. The spinnaker pole now dictates which gybe to stay on, because it is easier to flip the main boom back than to gybe the kite.

Gybing in strong winds

If it is very rough I prefer twin-pole gybing, because at the crucial moment both clews of the spinnaker are fixed to a pole so the sail can't sky, gyrate and cause a roll. Another advantage of the twin-pole system is that the babystay can be left on the whole time.

In strong winds it is doubly important to remind everyone to duck as the boom comes across, to make sure no one is in the way of the mainsheet and that there are no riding turns on the spinnaker sheets and guys.

If it is really howling consider lowering the kite before you gybe — it will lose less time than a broach in heavy seas. It is then a relatively simple matter to gybe the main and set another spinnaker. Note that there must enough stops to prevent the kite breaking out before it is fully hoisted.

Run-to-run gybes

So far we have been talking about reach-to-reach gybes. If you are gybing from run-to-run the same principles apply; the gybe will probably be easier although it is worth getting the boat as stable as possible before you begin. Settle her down by luffing a little or by pulling in the mainsheet: both of these damp any tendency to roll. Once she is steady get ready, and go . . .

14 · The leeward mark

There is plenty to do at the leeward mark. The kite comes down, the genoa is hoisted, the boat is steered round the buoy and the rig re-tuned. Naturally you can't do all of these at once, so I have listed below what needs to be done before the mark, and what can be left until you are safely round and on the beat.

Before the mark
Before the mark the navigator should carry out a 'wind on the next leg' calculation. From this you can choose the sails for the beat — let's say you decide on the number two genoa with one reef in the main.
- The crew boss informs the crew of the estimated time to the mark.
- Send two people forward to take off the old genoa and clip on the new one. Bear away slightly to compensate for their weight on the bows.
- Set the sheet leads for the new genoa.
- Reef the main or put in the flattener if required.
- Turn onto a run and hoist the genoa in good time. Leave it sheeted out (just off flapping) and adjust the halyard to its mark (it is easier to do this before the backstay and runners come on).
- Ease the spinnaker halyard a couple of inches (5 cm) to make sure it will run when the time comes. (We look later at what to do if it is stuck.)
- Set up the backstay and runners for the beat.
- Drop the spinnaker late (usually when you are level with the mark). The crew boss chooses the right moment, then the halyard is thrown off and the genoa wound in as the kite is gathered.
- Turn slowly, or the boat will stall (or broach).

Note that the pole is left up until you are on the beat, provided you are planning to stay on the same tack (if not, consider a float drop).

After the mark
- Tension the babstay.
- Fine-tune the genoa halyard.
- Adjust the mainsail controls.
- Lower the pole.

Sorting out disasters
So far we have been looking at what *should* happen. Unfortunately it doesn't always go like that, so let's see what can be done to sort out the most common blunders.

Spinnaker stuck. By letting off two to three inches (5 to 7 cm) of halyard well before the mark you can check whether the kite is going to come down cleanly. Sometimes the splice (or the ball) sticks in the mast sheave, in which case:
1. Bear off. Coming onto the run may free it.
2. Reduce mast bend by easing the backstay.
3. If neither of these do the trick, send a man up the mast to undo the halyard shackle. (If he can't get it undone he may have to saw through the head of the sail close to the eye — amazingly a sailmaker can sew on a new head patch quite easily.)

Everyone has his favourite story about spinnakers that refuse to come down; one of the most nerve-racking for me was during an inshore race in the Admiral's Cup. We were all set to round the leeward mark behind 'Robin' whom we had to beat to the line to win the race. Things always go wrong when you least want them to, and sure enough the spinnaker halyard picked this moment to jam itself firmly. We decided to ignore the advice I've been giving above,

Rounding the leeward mark: with a good crew there is no need to lower the spinnaker early — it can be dropped on rounding the buoy.

and to round the mark with the kite still up. Taking the guy around the genoa to the foot of the mast, we tripped the spinnaker and tacked — the sail now streaming back along the weather side of the main. This cost surprisingly little ground and a man was hauled aloft to cut the sail down; we were able to sort out the mess, pass 'Robin' and take the race.

Genoa won't go up. The usual reason for this is that the halyards are crossed. Try the next halyard!

Spinnaker in the water. The best ways to avoid dropping the kite in the water are:

- Take the lazy guy to a winch behind the main; in this way the spinnaker can't pull the retrieving line out of the crew's hands. Having the lazy guy forward keeps the kite in the lee of the main, and prevents it flagging out from the stern.
- Let the halyard go *fast* to the halfway point; the sail then floats down, and even if it hits the water tends to lie on top. If you let the halyard go slowly the spinnaker digs into the ocean and is a pig to get back on board. Trawling is a slow business at the best of times, and fresh fish are a poor substitute for boatspeed!

15 · Running

Many people see the run as a time to eat sandwiches and take off clothes — I must admit they have a point. It is so nice hurtling downhill in the sun that it is easy to forget the race, though good downwind technique will pull you past your rivals — especially if *they* are preoccupied with lunch.

Setting up the rig and sails

The boat goes fastest on the run with the mast straight and raked forwards. So reduce tension in the backstay and runners, but keep enough tension to stop the top of the mast bending forwards, and to prevent the rig flopping about in a seaway (it is embarrassing if all the pins are shaken out of the rigging).

Mainsail. The main needs to be baggy while still projecting the maximum area.
1. Let off the halyard and outhaul (to give draft). But if you are sailing dead downwind go for the maximum projected area.
2. Pull down on the vang sufficiently to keep the boom horizontal and prevent the main wrapping round the spreaders.

Spinnaker. The spinnaker is all-important.
1. Keep the pole horizontal (to project maximum area).
2. Set the pole as high on the mast as possible while still keeping the clews of the kite level. This is where many people go wrong — there is in fact a wide range of pole heights that keeps the clews even, but the fastest setting is with the pole at the top of that range.
3. Wind back on the guy to swing the pole as far aft as you can (without the sheet trimmer complaining too loudly). Aftest equals fastest, so the guy needs constant tending.
4. The sheet must constantly be eased to keep the luff of the spinnaker curling. Ease a foot, gain a yard — so keep the grinder sweating.

Blooper. On 'Yeoman' we fly a blooper if the wind is less than 40 degrees off the stern and in the range of 7 to 18 knots apparent. We reckon to gain up to 0.25 knots if the thing is properly working.

The secret is to set the sail as far to leeward of the main as possible. This is achieved by sheeting it over the top of the boom and easing the sheet and halyard

LEFT *'Jade'* has her mainsail controls well eased to give maximum draft. OPPOSITE In these conditions a blooper can add another quarter of a knot to your boatspeed.

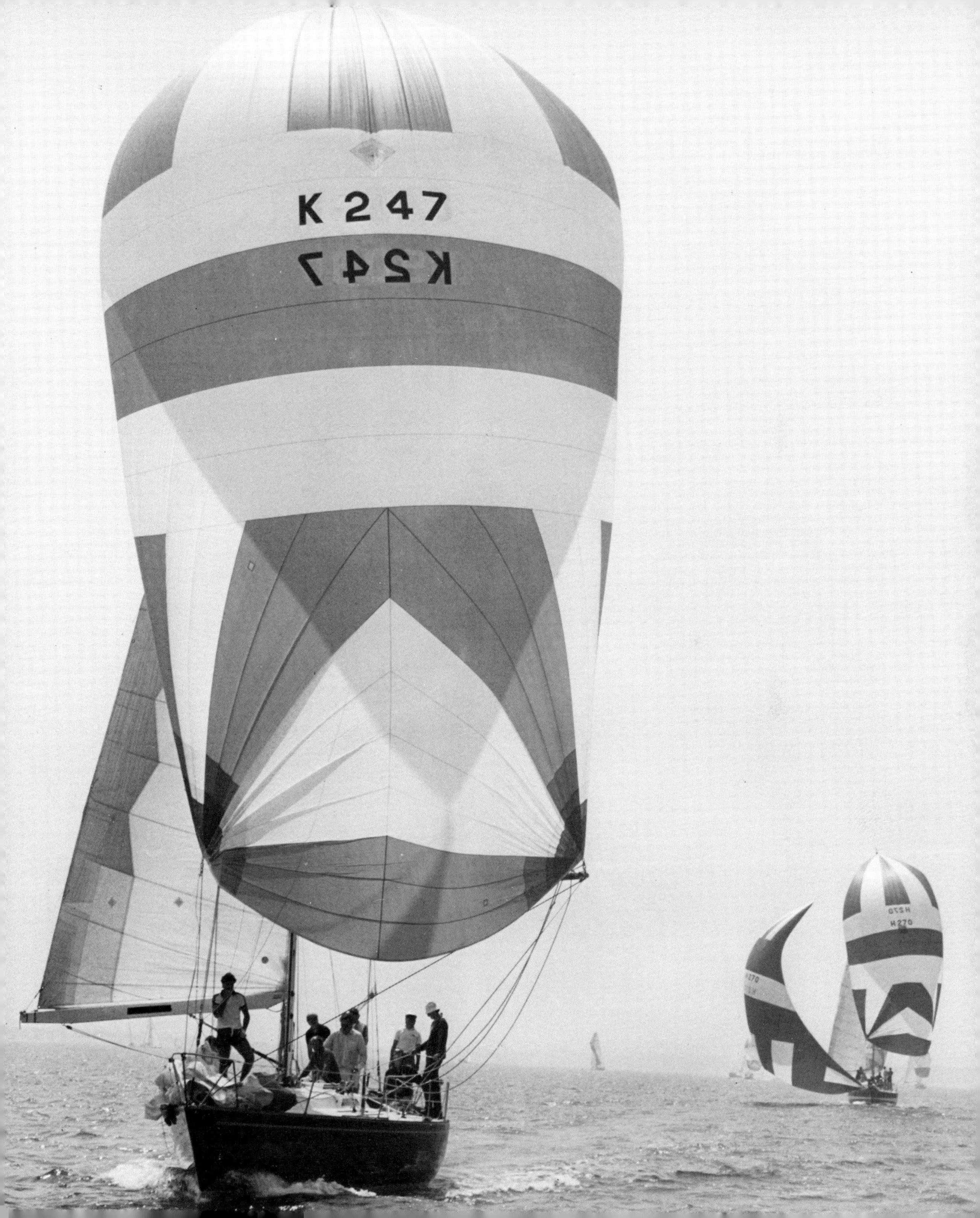
K 247
K247
H270

RUNNING

as far as possible while keeping the sail out of the water.

The blooper is a good stabiliser and helps prevent rolling; but the spinnaker is still the most important sail, so steer to it and play the blooper as best you can.

Trim

Always aim to trim the boat flat (side to side). Heeling only produces pressure on the helm, which slows you down. Except in light-to-medium airs don't heel the boat to weather, because of the danger of broaching (although heeling to windward *is* faster).

Make the crew sit down to reduce the rolling factor (you would never stand up in a dinghy on the run, and though a yacht is more stable ten heavies on the cabin roof can't possibly help).

In medium winds trim the boat flat fore-and-aft. In lighter airs push people forward to reduce wetted area, while in strong winds pull them aft to stabilise the boat.

Steering

If you are using a wheel stand on the centreline, feeling the roll of the boat through the balls of your feet.

Figure 15.1

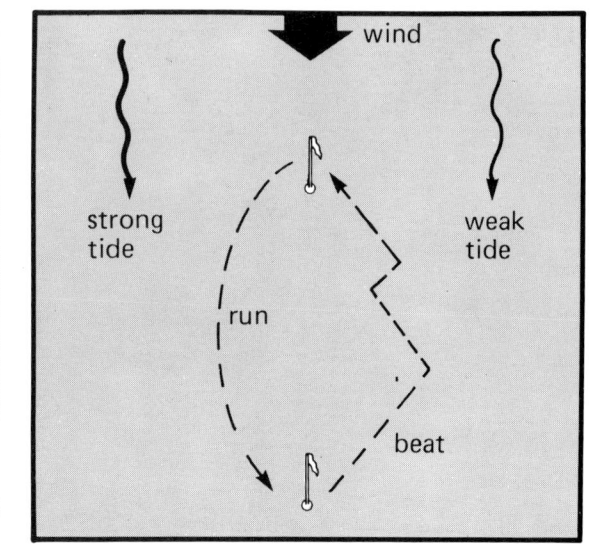

TOP *On the run, stand on the centreline with your feet braced.* BOTTOM *Marks on the mast help in positioning the spinnaker pole. In general it should be as high on the mast as will allow the clews to be level. It should also be horizontal and winched well aft.*

Although you can feel the wind on the back of your head, look frequently over your shoulder to check streaks of wind on the water (and to see how the opposition is faring). If you reckon there is a stronger patch over to one side, sail across towards it.

It is difficult to steer with a tiller on the run because you may need to luff suddenly (to avoid a wipe-out) and it is awkward pushing on the tiller extension. The best way round this is to sit on the windward deck but to have someone to leeward with his hands on the tiller — when you want to luff shout "pull".

If the waves are small, use the rudder as little as possible. Set up the rig for neutral helm: lift (which you needed on the beat) doesn't help downhill. If you have weather helm let out the mainsheet. Luffing a bit will cure lee helm.

Detail someone to watch for gusts approaching so you can bear off just before they arrive. Compensate by luffing in the lulls.

Which side of the rhumb line?

If one side of the beat was favoured, it is almost certain that you will go faster down one side of the run.

In figure 15.1 the right-hand side of the beat paid because the tide was weaker there, so sail down the other side on the run. In figure 15.2 the right-hand side of the beat was best because of a wind bend: in this case go to the same side of the run because this gives you the best wind angle on both port and starboard gybes.

Tacking downwind

No yacht sails well straight downwind, and you can increase her speed dramatically by luffing onto a broad reach. Although this takes you away from the rhumb line you can always gybe later and reach back to the leeward mark, a process known as tacking downwind. In figure 15.3 A follows this advice: although she sails further through the water than B her gain in speed more than compensates for the extra distance.

The secret is knowing how far to luff up — too little (C) and you gain no speed, too much (D) and you sail extra distance. Note that you have a similar decision to make on the beat — i.e. whether to pinch (and go slowly) or foot (and sail further from the mark).

Experience will tell you how far to luff, but a more

Figure 15.2

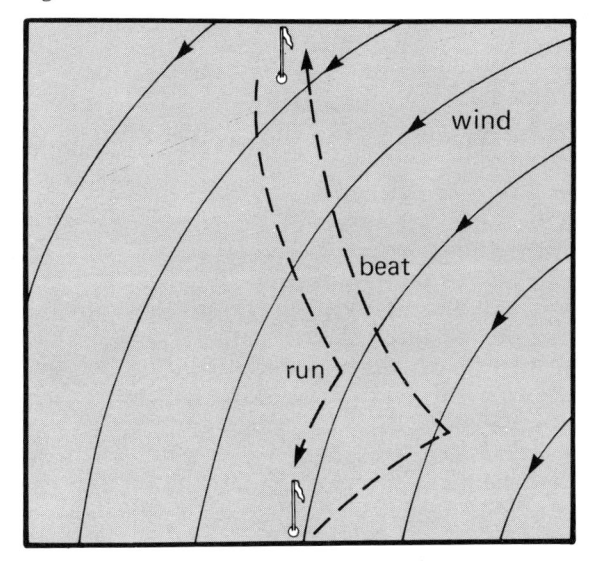

Figure 15.3

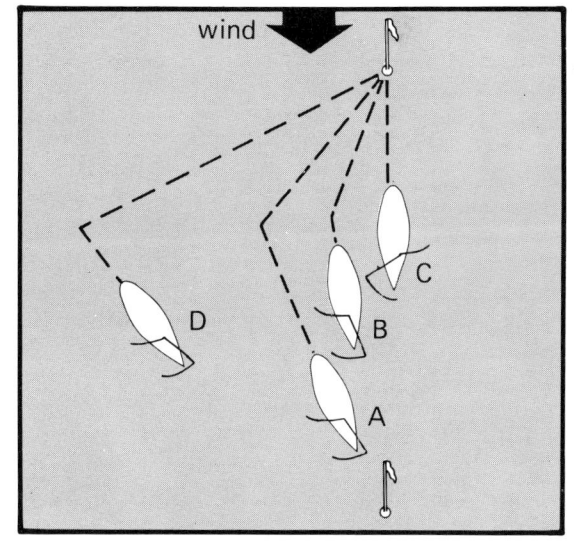

RUNNING

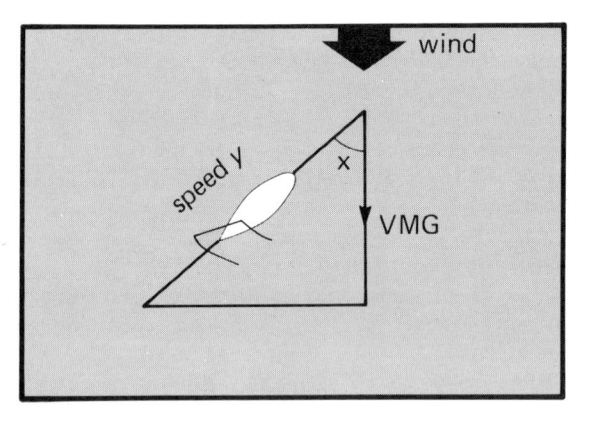

Figure 15.4

scientific method is to use a computer-generated polar table (see chapter 1) or to make one yourself during practice sessions. Simply sail at various angles to the wind and record your speed at each angle. For each pair of readings calculate the VMG (velocity made good) towards the leeward mark ($y \cos x$, figure 15.4) and then choose the angle that gives the best VMG. Alternatively, you can buy an expensive electronic box to do this for you!

You will find that in light winds it pays to come round much further — almost onto a beam reach — to gain what speed you can, while in strong winds the optimum course is only a few degrees off the rhumb line.

Gybing on the tide

If the tide is running across your course choose the gybe that puts the stream under your lee bow. If the tide turns during the leg then gybe as it turns. You can gauge this roughly from tide tables or more accurately using Decca: by plotting your course from the read-out you will see the track drifting one way and then the other. Gybe as it changes.

Gybing on windshifts

Windshifts are as important on the run as they are on the beat. I've described above how important it is to stay at the fastest angle to the wind; now let's see what happens as the wind shifts. In figure 15.5 the wind oscillates from side to side about a mean direction; note how E gybes on each shift while staying at the fastest angle to the current wind. F also stays at the fastest angle but doesn't gybe on the shifts, so her course weaves about and she makes poor progress.

Unfortunately it is difficult to spot shifts on the run. On 'Yeoman' the helmsman steers to the wind direction dial, while the tactician watches the compass heading. If the wind shifts so that we are heading further from the mark, then we gybe. On a light shifty day we might gybe once every ten minutes, even with the blooper on. The crew may not be crazy about it, but results prove the effort worthwhile.

Taking bearings

Boats often diverge on the run, and it is important to see if your choice of course is paying off. The only way to do this offshore is to take bearings on boats going the other way. I have found that binoculars with a built-in compass and range gauge are ideal for this: if the mast height of a boat behind appears to be increasing or if she is pulling angle on you, then her side of the course may be better, and you should consider gybing across towards her.

Wave riding

Apart from gybing downwind, wave riding is the best way to get ahead on the run. Planing on a big wave is not only exhilarating — you can add four or five knots to your speed if you catch it right.

1. Keep looking astern to spot suitable waves approaching.
2. If you see a steeper wave luff towards it (it seldom pays to bear off towards one because you lose speed on a dead run).
3. As the wave picks up your stern pump the spinnaker and the main sheets (check the rules to see what is legal here) and bear away.
4. If the boat accelerates too fast she will zoom straight into the trough and stop. If this begins to happen luff and steer along the wave face like a surfer. If your steering is good you can 'hang' on

the wave for up to half a mile — fantastic! Although this course is fast it takes you away from the rhumb line so you will eventually need to gybe and surf back the other way.

5 Once on a wave you will need to trim your sheets because the apparent wind comes ahead as you speed up.
6 If you have the opposite problem — i.e. the wind is not strong enough to keep the boat on the wave — head up and sheet in to increase speed.

The helmsman has no chance to steer to help the trimmers (because his main concern is catching each wave) so they are under even more pressure than usual to keep the luff of the main and kite just lifting.

Final checks

If we are going slowly relative to the polar table I generally check the following:
- Are the spinnaker clews the same height?
- Is the main in too tight?
- Is there weed around the prop? (You should have a spyhole for checking this.) If you turn the prop by hand the weed will wash off.
- Is there weed around the rudder? Clear this with a long-handled broom.

If we are going slowly relative to other boats then I look at:
- The tide (particularly if we are near the shore).
- Wind streaks. Often there are bands of wind along the shore — this is too large a subject to be dealt with here and is well covered in *Wind Strategy**.

Running in light airs

Move the crew forward and to leeward to reduce wetted area and help keep the sails full.

Set up the main with maximum bag on the foot and let off the halyard to give the sail a good draft (though after a certain point letting off the halyard simply loses area).

The main problem is getting up to speed — once

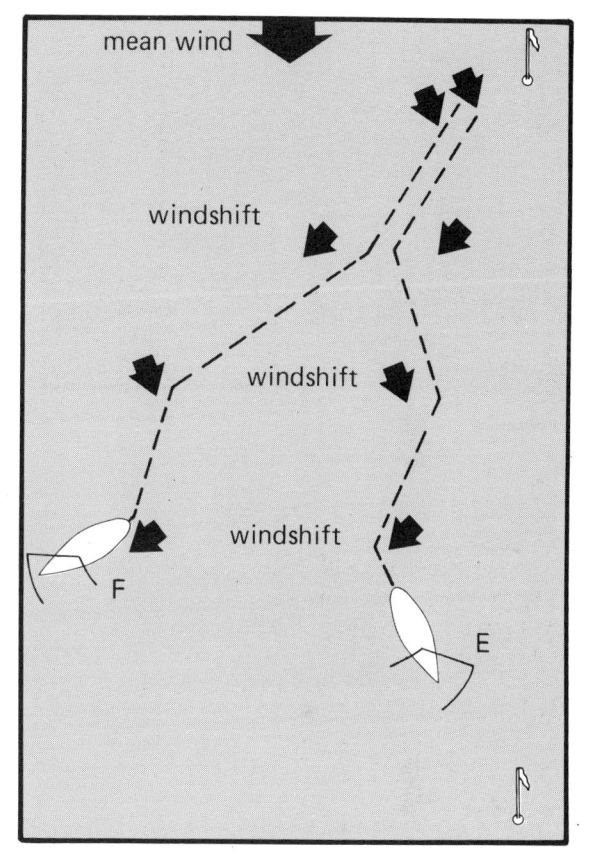

Figure 15.5

you are moving you create a certain amount of wind. In very light airs it is well worth tacking downwind at a frighteningly large angle to the rhumb line. To do this:

1. Come onto a broad (or even a beam) reach to pick up speed.
2. Slowly bear off watching the speedo and the wind angle. When the speed begins to drop straighten up and note the readings — say 3.7 knots at 110 degrees — and the VMG.
3. Ask the navigator to check this against the polar table to make sure you have got it right. Nine times out of ten he will tell you you are going too

* by David Houghton (Fernhurst Books).

On a run, keep the boat at the best angle to the wind and gybe on windshifts.

slowly ("We should be doing 4.2 knots") and have come off too far.
4 Repeat steps 1, 2 and 3 until you find the best angle for maximum VMG.

In light airs the tide is even more important than usual. Let's say the wind is 2 knots (true): a 2-knot tide in the right direction will double the apparent wind, while if it is in the wrong direction you will be wallowing in a flat calm. So if there is a patch of strong tide ahead make it work for you by crossing it on the better gybe (figure 15.6).

Running in strong winds

Running in a good blow is like driving at 120 mph on bald tyres: you get an interesting ride but when things go wrong it can be terminal. Here are a few suggestions for stabilising the boat and making the ride a little tamer.

Trim and rig
- Move the crew aft (behind the helmsman) and keep everyone low to prevent gyration. Trim the sails to keep the boat level.
- Set the vang tight to bow the mast and prevent it inverting.
- Rig a preventer to keep the boom out when the boat rolls; if the boom comes in too far it could keep going — an unplanned gybe is not recommended. The preventer should either be elastic or have a quick-release device so that if it comes under excessive load the boom can swing across to the other shroud. (A rigid preventer traps the boom to windward after a leeward broach. The boat then starts sailing backwards, the waves slop over the stern and begin to swamp her until eventually the preventer breaks and the boom scythes across the deck.)
- Have a jib on the bow ready to hoist. You may need it after a broach to pull the bow off the wind.

Spinnaker
Setting the kite in a strong breeze is always tricky. Steer virtually dead downwind and pull it up *well stopped* in the lee of the main and jib. Once it is set, keep control by bowsing down on the sheet and guy — the leads for both lines should be set right forward by the shrouds.

If you are not going to gybe for a while rig a spare halyard to the middle of the foredeck. This prevents the spinnaker wrapping itself round the forestay when the boat rolls.

Rolling
If you feel as though you are steering a waterbound pendulum:
- Pull in the main a little.
- Luff up a little.
- Bowse down the sheet and guy.
- Lower the spinnaker pole.

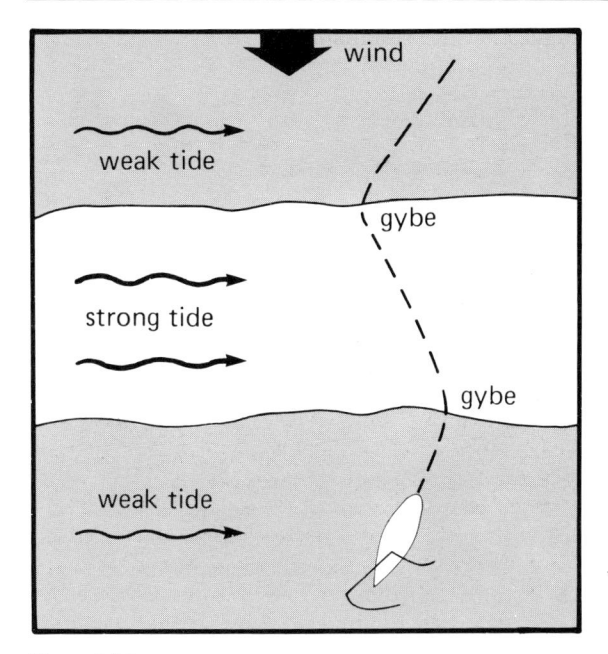

Figure 15.6

Broaching to leeward

Windward broaches are dealt with in chapter 12. On a run, however, it is also possible to broach to leeward — which is dangerous. If you think a broach is on the cards put in the washboards, close the hatch and warn the crew to keep low (the boom will come over pretty fast unless it is held by an elastic preventer).

The broach begins with a roll and the boat then skids along on the weather side of the hull. This flat shape makes her bear away more, centrifugal force brings the mast almost horizontal and eventually the boat gybes. Meanwhile the rudder has come out of the water and the helmsman is helpless. After the wipe-out:

1. Check the crew are still on board, are OK and that the mast is still in one piece.
2. The first job is to gybe the main by easing (or if neccessary cutting) the preventer. Make sure everyone's head is down. This is where a heavy-duty elastic preventer scores, as it automatically allows the boom across.
3. Pull on the new runner and let off the old one. The boat will now come upright with the spinnaker flagging out on the wrong side.

Decide whether you want to stay on the new gybe (which will inevitably involve dropping the kite to sort out the pole) or are you going to risk gybing the mainsail back (so you can keep the spinnaker flying). If you decide to stay on the new gybe:

- Take the lazy guy round the forestay to a winch.
- Wind in on the lazy guy to pull in the spinnaker behind the main, easing the sheet, guy and halyard.
- Sort out the pole, and prepare to re-hoist.

If you intend to gybe back, simply leave the spinnaker set, take a deep breath and put the helm up.

Very heavy air

In a real screamer you may decide that the kite is too dangerous. So pull it down and set a jib as a spinnaker (the number two is ideal).

Eventually you may decide to reef the main as well. This is difficult on the run because the sail wraps around the spreaders. Winding in the boom may help, but a strong grinder will still be needed.

In case you think we never have problems on 'Yeoman', I might mention an incident during last year's Seine Bay race. I was asleep in my bunk dreaming about standing under a waterfall when I came to and realised the dream was for real — water was *pouring* across the deck. Further sleep seemed unlikely so I climbed out of the hatch to find the blooper and spinnaker wrapped together around the forestay and the boat on her ear. Nothing seemed to budge the tangle and the crew were reluctant to destroy 2500 square feet of sail, so eventually the unfortunate owner was hoisted aloft clutching a breadknife. This proved an ideal weapon for hacking through both sails all the way down the forestay. I have to report that it hurt.

16 · Sailing at night

And then suddenly it all goes dark!

Most ocean races are won or lost at night. Time and again you will battle with another boat all day, only to leave her for dead during the night. The crew that can keep their concentration going, particularly around 0400 (when everyone is at his lowest pitch) will reap huge rewards.

I like sailing at night because that is when I feel closest to the boat and to the elements. One night I was steering down to leeward in light winds when a sparkling torpedo shot straight for me, veering aside at the last moment and surfacing as a porpoise. It barked playfully in my ear, then moved aside so the next in the school could buzz me. Fantastic.

Equipment

Before night falls check that all lines are in place, and that you know where everything is. Organise lifelines and lifejackets and bring hand-bearing compasses and torches on deck.

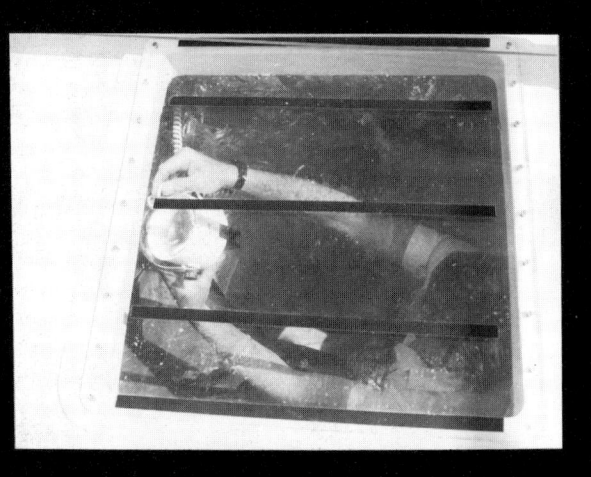

Batteries. Test the navigation and main compass lights — the battery should have been fully charged before the race, and should last through the first night before it needs recharging. But plan ahead: you can't run the engine when the boat is heeled, so if it is a run tonight with a beat tomorrow, recharge now. Some navigation equipment is sensitive to voltage variation, so if in doubt it is worth 'topping up'.

The current 'Yeoman' has six batteries but in future I plan to have three plus a generator, all positioned just above the keel (where their weight does most good).

Polar table. Although the polar table stays on deck all the time, it really comes into its own at night. How else can you judge whether or not you are up to speed?

Lights on the sails. We have several kinds of movable lights on board.
- Each crew member carries a small pocket torch for looking at sheet leads, reading the hydraulics and so on.
- We also have large rubber torches which will shine to the top of the mast to check crossed halyards, sail trim etc. One of these is used by the main trimmer.
- To light up the telltales on the genoa we have a 12-volt torch mounted on a swivel on the weather jib track. It is powered by the main battery via a wandering lead. (Some of my earlier boats had portholes in the deck with lamps underneath angled onto the telltales, but the

LEFT *Angle a lamp to light up the central pair of telltales on the genoa. It is essential to have a window in the genoa so the leeward telltale can be seen.*

later boats have sandwich core decks which are hard to cut holes in.)
- The light on the top of the mast is rigged to illuminate the Windex. I use this a lot because concentrating on the instruments alone is boring (and can send you to sleep).
- We keep an Aldis lamp handy down below and bring it on deck when shipping gets close — either to signal or just flash at them.

During sail handling we cut every light out and leave them off for as long as possible afterwards so no one can see what we have done. Similarly I don't like people flashing torches on the sails too often because it makes other crews curious: I prefer them to doze quietly and slip astern. But this isn't as subtle as one boat I know that had a rheostat on her stern light. This could be played for various effects; gradually dimming the light made people behind think they were dropping back (very demoralising), while turning it up could encourage a crew with the wrong sails to keep them set.

Lights below. The ideal is to have no lights on at all below; this is better both for those trying to sleep and for people on deck. We have a dual lighting system (red or white lights) and on the rare occasions when lights are needed tend to use the red.

As darkness falls

At dusk put the navigation lights on.

Taking bearings. Bring on deck the rubber-covered handbearing compasses: on our boat four crewmen have one and each monitors a boat we think is doing the right things. The bearings are taken throughout the night and jotted down on a piece of tape on the oilskin sleeve. We look for boats going faster than us (shown up by the change in bearing).
- Are they sailing in a stronger wind streak? Should we tack (or gybe) across to the streak?
- Have they tacked? If so, why? Has the tide turned?
- Are they sailing faster because they have more (or less) sail than us? Should we change sails?

Note that these compasses are also very useful for taking bearings on shipping to check if we are on a collision course.

Night sight. Your eyes gradually become accustomed to the dark, so even at 2300 you will find you can still see well. The objective is to leave all lights off as long as possible.

The instrument lights will be the first to go on — we use red lights, begin with them bright and gradually dim them as the night wears on. The lights on the sails come on later.

If you need to switch on a torch or cabin light warn everyone beforehand so they can shield their eyes, or they will lose their night sight.

Steering

The main problem when steering at night is disorientation. You may think you are on the wind when you aren't, and you tend to overestimate the windstrength because you are more receptive to noise. So use the instruments, particularly to prevent the boat being undersailed.

If I'm in the groove I stay on the helm up to four hours but if not, or if it is a windy downwind leg, two hours is plenty. To help combat tiredness *keep warm* — it is cold in that slot. Wear plenty of clothes, set off your ensemble with a Balaclava helmet (heat loss through the head is phenomenal), and have warm drinks as often as needed (more often than you think). Chocolate bars and biscuits to hand also help to top up the energy supply.

Judging changes in the wind and tide. It is the mainsheet trimmer's job to write down the wind direction and keep confirming it to the helmsman.

Although you can sometimes take bearings on buoys and lighthouses, the best way to judge tide changes at night is by watching the Decca. Failing that, tide tables will give an indication of what is going on (but remember the actual turn of the tide can be half an hour early or late depending on wind and atmosphere pressure).

Steering on the beat. You need a window near the genoa luff with telltales on each side — one higher than the other so you can tell which is which. Adjust the light so you can see the telltales clearly and sail to them. You will also find the angle-of-heel meter very useful.

Otherwise just sail as you would in daylight. Try to feel the boat over the waves, even though you can't see them. If you are helming as darkness falls this is easy because you just stay in the groove, but if you are taking over in the middle of the night the previous helmsman will help you (see below).

In fact a good crew can drive the boat to windward faster at night than in daylight because there are fewer distractions; we have exceeded the speeds on the polar table by more in the darkness than in daytime.

Steering downwind. When spinnaker reaching I tend not to sail as close as in daylight because it is easier to broach. Most crews overtrim the main and kite at night, so watch for this.

White-sail reaching at night is one of the most difficult skills. All you can do is experiment with the sheets and try to develop feel by watching the telltales on the genoa.

On the run I use the masthead Windex a lot. We sort out the boat's angle to the wind using the polar table and instruments and then note the Windex angle relative to its side arms. Then I steer to the Windex.

Sadly it is impossible to describe how to handle waves at night — as always it is a matter of feel, although you can often see breaking crests approaching.

It is difficult to ride the wake of a bigger boat in the dark but if you can catch a tow they may let you get away with it for a long time. 'Marionette', 'Victory' and 'Yeoman' were once towed most of the way from Brighton to Le Havre by a friendly yacht that was kind enough to sail straight through the pack. Needless to say they weren't quite so friendly when the corrected times were worked out.

Avoiding other yachts and shipping. From dusk till dawn the rules of the sea apply (as opposed to the racing rules) and most sensible people try to avoid collisions. You would not, for example, luff another boat in the dark.

The main problem is to tell how far away other boats are. In the middle of the night I have even mistaken a glowing cigarette end on the weather rail for a boat approaching on port — until a dollop of ash landed in my eye.

Big ships are the main danger. My recommendations are:

- Know your lights. We once passed between two ships a mile apart without realising one was towing the other. We got away with it but it is an experience I don't want to repeat.
- If in doubt always aim to pass *behind* a ship, not across her bows.
- If the bearing doesn't change you are on a collision course — tack or gybe to head away from her.
- If things get desperate *don't hesitate to use the engine* to keep clear. Enter this in the log and then carry on racing — there is a special provision in the rules and you won't be disqualified (and may not even be penalised).

Handing over to the next helmsman

While the new helmsman is waking up give the wheel to a third person, go below to the chart table and talk through your tactics, the weather forecast, what the wind has been doing and the estimated arrival time at the next mark (to prevent his getting caught downtide of the buoy).

Then go back on deck together, take the helm yourself and bring the boat back to full speed. Finally let the new helmsman take her, but stay with him until you are sure he is in the groove.

So what are the rewards of night racing? Throughout one night we had been in close touch with a much larger yacht, most of whose crew were asleep below. At dawn the three unfortunates on deck finally noticed us alongside.

"Bloody Yeoman", says one, "What's she doing up here?" And their mates were dragged on deck to get her going.

What better endorsement of a good night's sailing do you need?

17 · Offshore strategy

By the time you read this most boats will be using electronic navigation systems, and eventually I'm sure the chart will be displayed on a VDU, with a moving dot showing the boat's position.

Although it is wonderful to know exactly where you are, deciding which way to go next can never be solved by electronic means: for that you need experience, ability to interpret data . . . and luck!

Here are a few rules which I've found helpful in determining strategy for a long passage.

1 Sail the shortest distance through the water. When boat's logs are compared after the race the winner's almost always has the lowest reading.

2 Sail near the rhumb line. The rhumb line is the direct course over the ground. We seldom sail along it because one side is usually favoured. On the other hand we always try to stay inside a 10-degree 'cone' drawn around the rhumb line (see figure 11.1, p. 64). Once outside this, you risk sailing extra distance through the water (contravening my first rule).

3 Deduce windshifts from the weather map. The wind seldom stays constant on a long leg. Try to predict which way the breeze will swing, then head towards the new wind.

If it is going to turn into a beat head up as high as possible early on. Note how A in figure 17.1 pulls ahead of B, who ends up downwind of the mark.

If you get caught by an unexpected shift *don't* make things worse by taking a flyer outside the 10-degree cone. In figure 17.2 the plan was to gybe downwind, but a shift leaves C in a dilemma: should she keep her kite up and head out to port, or drop it and fetch back towards the rhumb line? The second course is by far the safest.

Figure 17.1

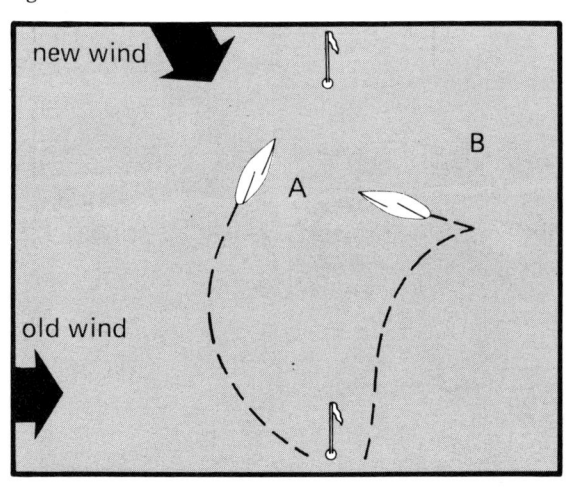

Figure 17.2

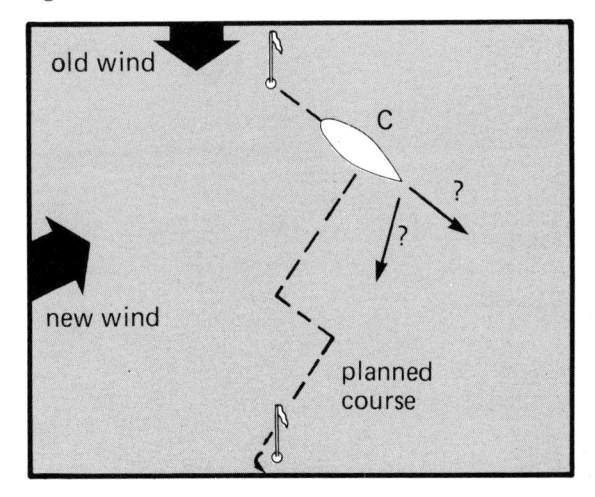

OFFSHORE STRATEGY

4 Don't arrive downtide of the next mark. And never place yourself downtide *and* downwind of it — beating into the stream is no fun.

5 On a beat, stay on the making tack. Suppose you sail at 40 degrees to the true wind. If your course is less than 40 degrees off the mark, stay on your present tack. In practice the navigator should give you a bearing for this: "If you head more than 290 degrees, tack".

Note that you do not necessarily need to tack on a header: if you are pointing at the mark and a 30 degree header comes through *carry on* — you are still on the making tack.

6 Tack on the tide. If you are beating in a crosstide aim to keep the tide under your lee bow. The boat in figure 17.3 sets off on starboard, tacks onto port as the tide turns and is pushed upwind by the tide on both tacks. To be safe she should, in fact, tack before the tide turns to make sure she arrives uptide of the next mark (see rule 4).

7 Gybe on the tide. The boat in figure 17.4 increases her apparent wind by choosing her gybe to match the tide.

8 Beware of land masses. If the next mark is near the land listen to the local radio forecast. If you are racing to a foreign shore have someone on board who speaks the language. If, for example, they forecast hot sun on the beach you might expect a sea breeze (or a land breeze later that night).

9 Consider speed differences later in the leg. Let's say the passage in figure 17.5 is estimated to take six hours at our current speed of eight knots. So there will be a net westerly tide for two hours. What course should we steer as we leave A?

The answer is to lay off to the east immediately. If the wind decreases we will slow down, spend more than four hours in the westerly tide, and need every yard gained up tide of the mark. If the wind increases, on the other hand, we won't go much faster (eight knots is near our maximum speed) so we will still be on course.

Figure 17.3

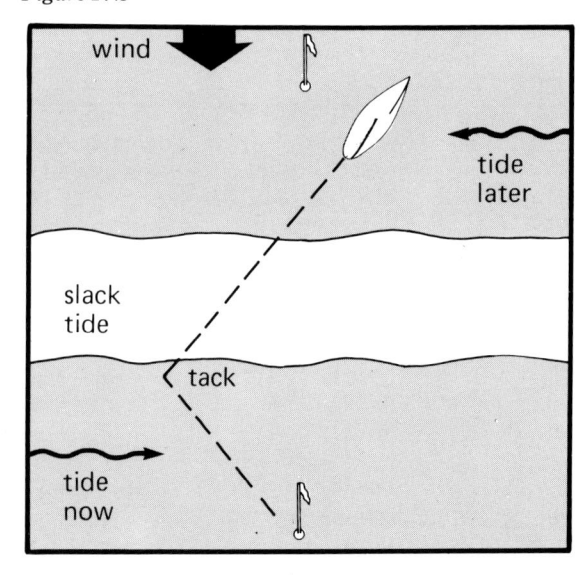

Figure 17.4

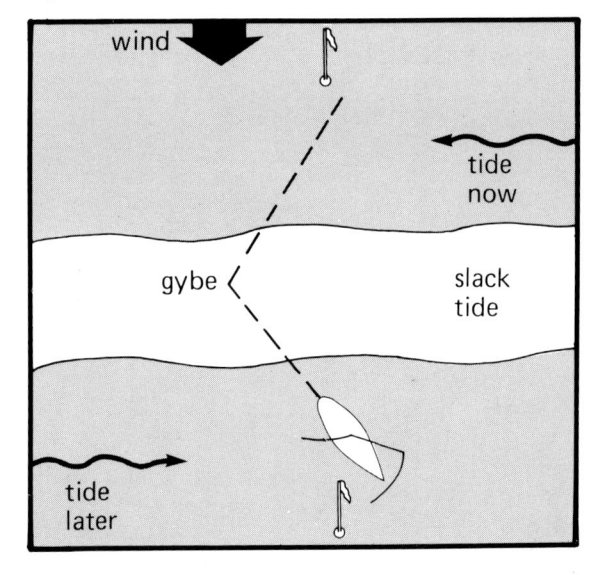

An illustrious addition to 'Yeoman's' crew: HRH the Duke of Edinburgh on board during Cowes Week.

Figure 17.5

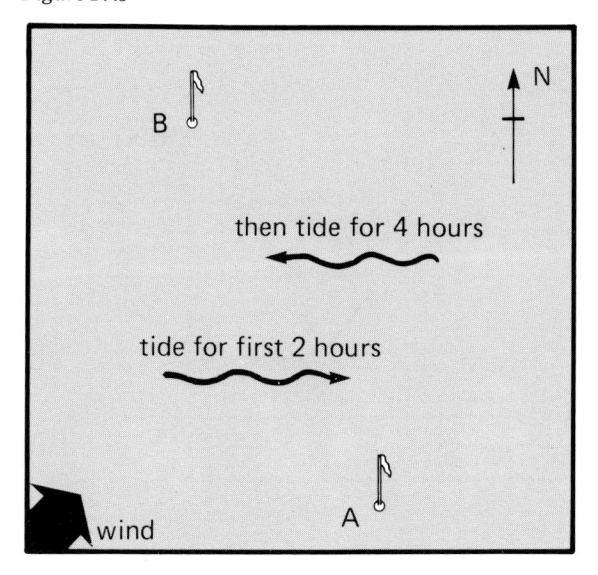

10 Calculate your course VMG. Having worked out the optimum course you may find that luffing or bearing away a few degrees gives more speed; maybe you can catch the waves better, or hoist the kite. My advice is to try it, then calculate whether the gain in speed is worth the extra distance covered.

Do beware, however, of a temporary gain putting you downtide or downwind of the next mark.

11 Sail the fleet. If the whole fleet has just disappeared to the left and you're still steadfastly heading right, double and triple check your strategy. Surely they can't all be wrong?

12 Never hesitate to call the navigator. Often you have a gut feeling that there is going to be a change in the weather, the wind or the tide. Cocooned

OFFSHORE STRATEGY

SAILING FROM X TO Y OFFSHORE	DEAD RUN (wind from Y toward X)	BROAD REACH	REACH (just too close for spinnaker)	CLOSE REACH
NO TIDE	1. Tack downwind at the fastest angle.	7. Sail rhumb line.	13. Set kite and bear off. Drop kite later and close reach up to mark.	19. Sail rhumb line.
WIND EXPECTED TO VEER	2. If large veer expected soon, set off on port. If small veer expected later, set off on starboard and gybe on the shift.	8. Small veer—sail straight. Large veer—luff a little.	14. Luff early.	20. Luff as high as possible. After veer stay on port until this becomes losing tack—then tack.
WIND EXPECTED TO BACK	3. Opposite to (2).	9. Begin on port, gybe on the shift.	15. Put kite up now and bear off.	21. Sail straight and prepare to set kite.
TIDE TO RIGHT	4. Start on port gybe in case wind drops later. If the tide will turn during the leg, set off on starboard then gybe on the tide.	10. Steer the heading required for rhumb line course.	16. Danger of being swept downtide. Luff onto close reach; set kite later.	22. Steer heading required for rhumb line course.
FOLLOWING TIDE	5. As (1).	11. As (10).	17. As (13) but drop kite early.	23. Sail straight
ADVERSE TIDE	6. As (1).	12. As (10).	18. As (13) but drop kite late.	24. Sail straight.

Figure 17.6

OFFSHORE STRATEGY

in electronic gadgetry, the navigator may have missed the signs. Wake him and ask him to rework his calculations until you are sure you are going the right way.

The table in figure 17.6 shows how these rules can be applied to various combinations of wind and tide. In each case the yacht is sailing from X to Y.

Sailing around headlands

The tide is modified dramatically as it flows around a headland, so on coastal legs plan ahead carefully to make best use of each shore feature. Remember:

- The tide turns first inshore.
- The tide runs strongest close to a headland (figure 17.7) because the water funnels fast past the obstruction. There is, however, a small patch of slack water extending a short distance from the shore (due to frictional effects).
- There may be a back eddy downtide of the headland.
- If there is a bay on either side of the headland the wind will be light in the bay.

ONE-SIDED BEAT	BEAT
25 Sail the long leg first.	**31** Keep within the 'funnel' and play the windshifts.
26 Keep on port. Tack when starboard becomes the making tack.	**32** Port tack, starboard after shift.
27 Port tack.	**33** Starboard tack, port after shift.
28 Port tack.	**34** Starboard tack (takes you closer to mark).
29 Port tack.	**35** As (31). Beware of overstanding.
30 Port tack.	**36** As (31).

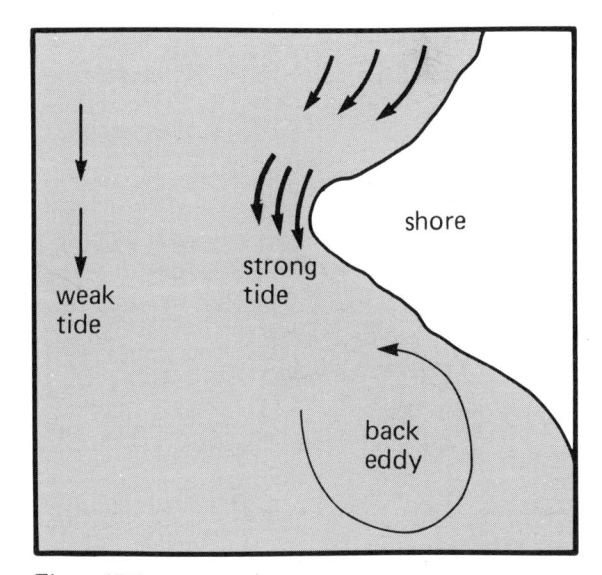

Figure 17.7

So when sailing around a headland:
1. Sail offshore if the tide is against you.
2. Sail inshore if the tide is with you.
3. Beware if the tide is about to turn.

Suppose you are approaching a headland with the tide, but you expect it to turn shortly. By going out to sea you may get through (the tide turns later offshore). If this fails (or you reach the headland later than expected) you have two choices. Either sail right inshore to catch the back eddy in the bay and then cheat the tide close to the headland. Alternatively head well offshore where the tide is weaker.

On the Fastnet race there are several headlands, each of which may act as a tidal gate in this way. One year we arrived at Portland Bill at night with a foul tide, and decided to go inshore. Sure enough there was a band of slack water, but it only extended 15 feet (5 metres) out from the rocks; beyond this there was a foul four-knot current. 'Yeoman' was unceremoniously short-tacked along the shore like a dinghy, much to the annoyance of the fishermen on the point — who didn't seem too interested in the outcome of the Admiral's Cup. Gradually we got the hang of it — inshore until the keel hit, tack, then tack back and wait for the next bump. Finally, under a barrage of mussels from our friends on the cliffs, we rounded the headland and settled down to some less gymnastic sailing in Lyme Bay.

Other books in the 'Fernhurst Offshore' series

Yacht Crewing *by Malcolm McKeag*
Yacht Tuning *by Lawrie Smith* (in preparation)

'Sail to Win' series

Tactics *by Rodney Pattisson*
Wind Strategy *by David Houghton*
The Rules in Practice *by Bryan Willis*